Science, Grade 1

Table of Contents

Unit 3: Life Science

Answer Key

Introduction

Children see the world around them and ask questions that naturally lead into the lessons that they will be taught in science. Science is exciting to children because it answers their questions about themselves and the world around them—their immediate world and their larger environment. They should be encouraged to observe their world, the things in it, and how things interact. A basic understanding of science boosts students' understanding of the world around them.

Organization

Science provides information on a variety of basic science concepts. It is broken into three units: Physical Science, Earth and Space Science, and Life Science. Each unit contains concise background information on the unit's topics, as well as exercises and activities to reinforce students' knowledge and understanding of basic principles of science and the world around them.

This book contains three types of pages:

- Concise background information is provided for each unit. These pages are intended for the teacher's use or for helpers to read to the class.

- Assessments are included for use as tests or practice for the students. These pages are meant to be reproduced.

- Activity pages contain information on a subject, or they list the materials and steps necessary for students to complete a project. Questions for students to answer are also included on these pages as a type of performance assessment. As much as possible, these activities include most of the multiple intelligences so students can use their strengths to achieve a well-balanced learning style. These pages are also meant for reproduction for use by students.

Use

Science is designed for independent use by students who have been introduced to the skills and concepts described. Copies of the activities can be given to individuals, pairs of students, or small groups for completion. They may also be used as a center activity. If students are familiar with the content, the worksheets may also be used as homework.

Hands-On Experience

An understanding of science is best promoted by hands-on experience. *Science* provides a wide variety of activities for students to do. But students also need real-life exposure to their world. Playgrounds, parks, and vacant lots are handy study sites to observe many of nature's forces and changes.

It is essential that students be given sufficient concrete examples of scientific concepts. Appropriate manipulatives can be bought or made from common everyday objects. Most of the activity pages can be completed with materials easily accessible to the students.

Suggestions for Use

- **Bulletin Board:** Display completed work to show student progress.

- **Portfolios:** Have your students maintain a portfolio of their completed exercises and activities or of newspaper articles about current events in science. This portfolio can help you in performance assessment.

- **Assessments:** Use the overall and unit assessments as diagnostic tools by administering them before students begin the activities. After students have completed each unit, let them retake the unit test to see the progress they have made.

- **Center Activities:** Use the worksheets as a center activity to give students the opportunity to work cooperatively.

- **Fun:** Have fun with these activities while you and your students uncover the basic principles of science.

FOSS Correlation

The Full Option Science System™ (FOSS) was developed at the University of California at Berkeley. It is a coordinated science curriculum organized into four categories: Life Science; Physical Science; Earth Science; and Scientific Reasoning and Technology. Under each category are various modules that span two grade levels. The modules for this grade level are highlighted below.

Physical Science
- Solids and Liquids: 15–23, 25–28
- Balance and Motion: 31–41, 44–46

Earth Science
- Pebbles, Sand, and Silt: 71–82
- Air and Weather: 86–98, 104, 112

Life Science
- Plants: 125–138
- Insects: 125, 139, 142, 151, 152, 154, 155, 156

Overall Assessment

📦 **Read each sentence. Circle <u>true</u> or <u>false</u>.**

1. Solids do not have a shape.	true	false
2. Milk is a liquid.	true	false
3. Air is a gas.	true	false
4. A scale tells how long something is.	true	false
5. A magnet can pick up paper.	true	false
6. Gravity pulls things toward the ground.	true	false

📦 **Read each sentence. Circle <u>yes</u> or <u>no</u>.**

7. It takes more force to lift the small drum.   yes   no

8. It is easier to ride down the hill.   yes   no

GO ON TO THE NEXT PAGE 👉

Overall Assessment, p. 2

□ **Which word makes the sentence true? Circle it. Then, write the word in the sentence.**

_____

9. Plants grow in _____.

soil   clouds   stars

_____

10. You cannot see _____.

rocks   air   water

_____

11. Moving air is called _____.

Sun   soil   wind

_____

12. We get light and heat from the _____.

Moon   Sun   stars

_____

13. Clouds look _____ when it rains.

light   short   dark

GO ON TO THE NEXT PAGE ☞

Overall Assessment, p. 3

 Circle the living things.

14.

 Write <u>A</u> for animal or <u>P</u> for plant under each thing.

15.

_____ _____ _____ _____

 Circle the mammal. Draw a line under the fish. Draw an <u>X</u> on the bird. Draw a triangle around the reptile. Draw a square around the insect.

16.

 Circle the foods that are good for you.

17.

Unit 1: Physical Science

BACKGROUND INFORMATION

Matter

Matter is all around. It is everything that we see and touch. Moreover, matter has mass, or weight, and takes up space. Matter is identified in three forms: solid, liquid, and gas. Though students can easily comprehend and recognize the properties of a solid and liquid, it is generally difficult for them to understand that air is matter. Students begin to grasp this complex concept as they explore what air is and that it takes up space.

Matter can be easily described by its properties, both physical and chemical. Physical properties describe how a substance looks, which includes color, shape, texture, melting point, and boiling point. By using their senses, students can describe what an item looks and feels like. Chemical properties tell how something reacts with another substance so that it changes in its appearance, taste, or smell. For example, iron reacts with oxygen and water to make a new substance, rust.

All matter is made up of tiny particles called molecules. Molecules are made up of even smaller particles called atoms. Molecules cannot be seen with a microscope, but students can understand a substance's properties by using their senses when performing simple experiments. If sugar is dissolved in water, the sugar cannot be seen; but it can be detected through taste because the water is sweet. By using the sense of smell, students can identify molecules of

vinegar in air, a gas. To some degree, hearing can be used to sense molecules, because a smoke detector detects molecules of smoke in the air and buzzes to alert people to the potential danger.

Solids

The state of matter is determined by the density of the molecules and how fast they move. In a solid, the molecules are attracted to each other and are tightly held together. The movement of the particles is limited; they vibrate only. Therefore, a solid has a definite shape and volume. For example, a rock has a certain shape. It can be broken into smaller pieces, but its molecules do not change. A solid's mass is measured in grams (g), a metric weight that is a scientific measurement standard.

Liquids

Liquids have a definite volume, but they take the shape of the container. The molecules in a liquid are not packed as tightly, so they can move about more freely and easily by sliding over each other. This movement is what makes a liquid take the shape of the container. When juice is in a carton, it takes the shape of the carton. Yet if poured into a glass, the juice takes the shape of the glass. The volume of a liquid is measured in milliliters (mL), the scientific standard measurement for liquid.

Gas

Gas is the third state of matter. It is harder for students to understand the properties of gas, because they cannot see it, nor have they had exposure to different kinds of gases. In a gas, the molecules are far apart and move very quickly and randomly in all directions. They bounce off each other when they collide. Gas has no definite shape or volume. Gas, therefore, expands to take the shape of a container. Gas is also measured in milliliters (mL).

Changes in Matter

All matter can change form, meaning it can change from one state to another. When matter changes, nothing is lost or gained; the molecules stay the same. The addition or the removal of heat causes the molecules to get closer or farther apart. Moreover, the greater the amount of heat, the faster the molecules move. These changes in the density and the speed of a substance's molecules cause the state of matter to change.

When a solid is heated, the molecules expand. The heat causes the speed and volume of molecules to change. They vibrate faster and slip out of position, resulting in the solid changing into a liquid. This process is called melting, and the point at which the solid changes to a liquid is called the melting point. All matter, including rocks, has a melting point. The most commonly recognized melting point (or freezing point) is that of water, which is 0° on the Celsius scale or 32° on the Fahrenheit scale. Even with this change, the structure of the molecules stays the same.

When a liquid is heated, the loose molecules continue to expand. The vibration increases, causing them to collide with each other and move in all directions. When the boiling point is reached, the liquid changes into a gas. (The most commonly recognized boiling point is that of water. It boils at 100° Celsius or 212° Fahrenheit.) This process is called evaporation. Again, the molecules stay the same; nothing is lost or gained when the matter changes states.

The removal of heat causes the reverse changes in matter. Through condensation, a gas is cooled, and the molecules contract. They stop colliding and return to their loosely packed state, thus becoming a liquid. If heat is removed to the point that a liquid reaches its freezing point, a liquid will become a solid. The molecules are densely packed and cannot slide around. In any of these changes, nothing is lost or gained; only the properties of matter change.

Students can easily experiment with changes in states by watching ice change to water and steam. Ice is a solid, but when heated to its melting point, turns to liquid water. No water is lost or gained in the process, and no molecules are changed. When more heat is added, the water begins to boil and changes to a gas called water vapor. The gas cannot be seen because it has no color. Again, no water is lost or gained, and the molecules stay the same. If a spoon is held in the water vapor, the surface temperature of the spoon, which is room temperature, causes the water vapor to cool and condense back to liquid water. Likewise, by removing the heat and freezing the water, it changes states again to become ice.

Physical Changes

Matter can be changed in two ways, either in a physical change or in a chemical change. A physical change in matter is a change in which the molecules of a substance or substances do not change. There are three kinds of physical change. When matter changes states, as explained above, it is one kind of physical change.

A second kind of physical change takes place when a mixture is made. A mixture is a combination of substances in which the molecules of the substances diffuse evenly. Each substance retains its own properties and can be detected by the senses. No molecules are lost, gained, or changed. Moreover, a mixture can be separated by physical means, such as filtering, sorting, heating, or evaporating.

Each state of matter can make a kind of mixture. A fruit salad is an example of a solid mixture easily explained to students. Students can see and taste each piece of fruit. Sorting the fruit chunks is possible. Gas can also be mixed with another substance to form a mixture. The scent of a flower mixes with air so that you can smell the flower a few meters away. You use your sense of smell to become aware of the scent. A liquid can also be made into a mixture. Often a solid is dissolved into a liquid. This kind of mixture is called a solution. It is hard to separate out the parts, but it can be done. Lemonade is a good example to explain a solution. Water, lemon, and sugar are mixed together. Even though lemonade does not look like a mixture, the ingredients can be separated. The lemon can be filtered out. The water can evaporate, leaving crystals of sugar.

A third kind of physical change takes place when the shape of a substance is changed through cutting, ripping, or grinding. A log can be cut into many pieces. What remains are sawdust and cut logs. The molecules of the log itself have not changed.

Chemical Changes

When the molecules of a substance change, a chemical change has taken place. A new substance is always made in a chemical change, but molecules are never lost. Even though new molecules are made, the same number of atoms exists. Energy, generally in the form of heat, causes the atoms in molecules to form different molecules. Baking is a common example of a chemical change. Sugar, milk, eggs, and flour are combined to make a cake batter mixture. When heat is added, a chemical change takes place to turn the ingredients into a cake. Chemical changes also occur in the human body. Through chemical changes, food and oxygen react in the body's cells to create energy to make the body work.

Force

A force is simply a push or a pull. There are magnetic forces and gravitational forces, but in this unit, students will explore what force and gravity are. Forces can be balanced or unbalanced, and it is the interaction of these kinds of forces that creates motion. If forces are balanced, there is no movement. For example, if a kite is not moving while you are flying it, the force of the wind is balancing the weight of the kite and the pull of the string. However, if the wind stops blowing, the weight of the kite and the pull of the string would be greater, causing the forces to become unbalanced. The kite would then move.

Forces also differ in size and direction. To move a book takes a small amount of force, but to move a bookshelf would take much more force. Forces can also come from up, down, left, and right. Sometimes it is hard for students to understand that when they are pushing or pulling an object, even though the object does not move, force is present.

Gravity

Gravity is a force that attracts all objects that have mass. It is the force that keeps all objects from flying off the surface of the Earth. It is also the force that keeps the planets, Moon, and stars in orbit. Everything on the Earth is pulled to the center of the Earth by this unseen force. Calling the force *gravitation*, Sir Isaac Newton explained that all things have force but that the pull of the Earth is greater than that of other objects. Thus, gravity anchors objects to the Earth's surface and makes things fall down. The more massive an object, the greater the force that will be exerted. The force of gravitation is about 9.8 newtons per kilometer for every object on Earth.

Gravitational force depends on the mass of an object and how far apart the centers of the objects are. The more mass an object has, the greater the gravitational pull will be. The gravitational force between the Earth and other objects is greater because the mass of the Earth is so large. If the mass of two objects is small, the gravitational force will also be small because the force of the Earth's gravity is greater. For example, if two books are side by side on a table, they will stay on the table because of the pull of gravity from Earth. If the forces of gravity and friction were not working, the books would move toward each other.

Furthermore, the farther apart the bodies are, the less the pull will be because less force can be exerted.

Motion

The motion of an object is the result when a variety of forces interact. A change in motion occurs if a still object moves or an object already in motion changes speed or direction. Two equal forces, acting in opposite directions, will interact so an object will not move. These forces are considered balanced forces. An unbalanced force results when a force is placed on an object either at rest or in motion, making the object change its state. The object will move faster as the forces become more unbalanced.

Suppose a soccer ball is on the field. It is in a state of rest; the forces are balanced. But if someone kicks the ball, the force of the kick makes the ball move. The greater the force, the faster the ball will go, and the farther it will go. But there is more to motion than just force. The movement of an object is also affected by friction, the force that resists movement.

Friction

Friction is a force that keeps resting objects from moving and tends to slow motion when one object rubs against another object. Moreover, heat is produced as objects rub across each other. Early humans used the force of friction to make fire when they rubbed two sticks together.

Every motion is affected by friction. It is useful when movement needs to be slowed but can cause problems when something heavy needs to be moved. An object's surface affects the amount of friction it produces. Rough surfaces, like concrete, dirt, and grass, create more friction. Rough surfaces can help people walk without sliding. Smooth surfaces, like ice and lacquered wood, have less friction, so motion is easier. They can, however, cause motion to accelerate too quickly.

Mass and surface areas of objects affect the amount of friction. The heavier an object is, the greater the amount of friction. By lightening the load, you can decrease the friction, and the load can be moved easily with less force. Similarly, when large surface areas come into contact during motion, friction is greater. By reducing the contact of the surface areas, one can move an object more easily.

In many cases, friction can be reduced by using wheels. There will be less friction because the surface area is less and the surface area that rubs against the floor moves with the load. Lubricants, materials like oil or soap, also aid in friction reduction. Lubricants coat the surface of an object to decrease rubbing. Machines need lubricants to reduce the friction when parts rub against each other. This helps to keep the parts cool to avoid fire hazards as well as to keep them moving smoothly.

Magnetism

Magnetism is a force that attracts metal materials like iron, steel, nickel, and cobalt. The force is found in magnets, naturally found in the rock lodestone. They attract, or pull, and repel, or push, other pieces of metal. Synthetic magnets are made from steel or a combination of aluminum, nickel, cobalt, and iron. It is easy to transfer a magnetic charge to iron, but the charge will not last. Proper storage of synthetic magnets is important for them to retain their force.

Magnets come in all shapes and sizes. The force is focused at the ends, or poles, of the magnets. All magnets have a north pole and a south pole; most magnets are marked with an *N* and an *S* at the ends. (However, if the poles are not marked on a bar magnet, hang the magnet from a string. The north end of the magnet will point toward the north.) Like ends of two magnets repel each other. In other words, if two north ends of magnets were held together, they would repel each other. Unlike ends, a south and a north end, would attract each other. The area between the poles has some magnetic force, too, but it is not as strong as the poles.

Magnets do not need to touch, though. There is a magnetic force around each magnet called a magnetic field. When a piece of metal comes within a certain distance of the magnet, the magnet's field starts to pull the metal. The pull increases as the metal gets closer to the magnet. The size of the magnet affects the strength of the magnetic field.

Compasses

Compasses have been used for centuries to locate positions. Even before compasses were invented, people used rocks known for their iron content to point the way north. Compasses work because the Earth acts like a giant magnet. It has a north and south pole. The magnetic north pole is located in Canada. Different theories suggest why that part of Earth has this magnetic force. One theory is that iron and nickel in the core of the Earth create the magnetic field. Others believe that the rotation of the Earth and the electric currents in the Earth's atmosphere cause the force.

Electromagnets

As electric charges move through a wire, a magnetic field is created around the wire. It is this force that is used to make an electromagnet. A metal bar is wrapped in wire and connected to an electric source, such as a dry cell. The more wire used, the greater the magnetic field and the stronger the magnet is. Doorbells and cranes in junkyards use the energy of electromagnets.

RELATED READING

- *How Tall, How Short, How Faraway* by David A. Adler (Holiday House, 1999).

- *Like a Windy Day* by Frank Asch (Gulliver, 2002).

- *Magnets* by Angela Royston (*My World of Science Series*, Heinemann, 2001).

- *Metal* by Chris Oxlade (*Materials, Materials, Materials Series*, Heinemann, 2002).

- *A Perfect Day for It* by Jan Fearnley (Harcourt, 2002).

- *Pop! A Book About Bubbles* by Kimberley Brubaker Bradley (*Let's-Read-and-Find-Out Science Series*, HarperCollins, 2001).

- *Push and Pull* by Jack Challoner (*Start-Up Science Series*, Raintree Steck-Vaughn, 1996).

- *Roller Coaster* by Marla Frazee (Harcourt, 2003).

- *Water* by Frank Asch (Gulliver, 1995).

- *What Does a Wheel Do?* by Jim Pipe (Copper Beech, 2002).

- *What's Smaller Than a Pygmy Shrew?* by Robert E. Wells (Whitman, 1995).

Unit 1 Assessment

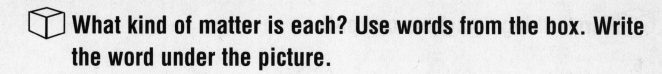 **What kind of matter is each? Use words from the box. Write the word under the picture.**

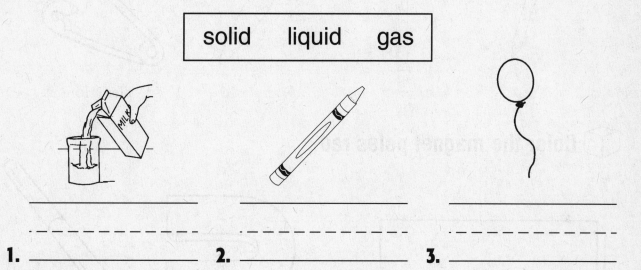

| solid | liquid | gas |

1. _____   2. _____   3. _____

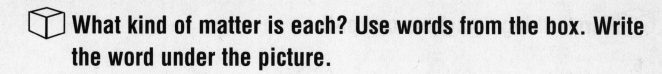 **Choose the word that answers: What am I? Write the word on the line.**

| gravity | force |

4. I pull things down. What am I?

_____

I am _____ .

5. You need me to lift things. What am I?

_____

I am _____ .

GO ON TO THE NEXT PAGE ☞

Unit 1 Assessment, p. 2

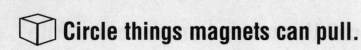 **Circle things magnets can pull.**

6.

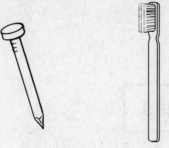  

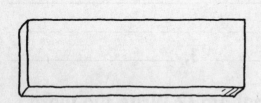 **Color the magnet poles red.**

7.

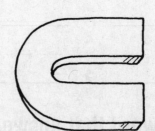 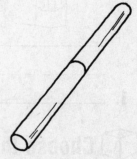

🔲 **Write push or pull next to each pair.**

8. | S   N | | N   S | _____

9. | N   S | | S   N | _____

10. | S   N | | S   N | _____

Look at Matter

All things are made of **matter**. You can tell about matter.

 Look at each picture. Which word tells about it? Draw a line from a word to a picture.

hard		**1.** 
soft		**2.** 
rough		**3.** 
smooth		**4.** 
shiny		**5.** 
dull		**6.**

Tell About Matter

You can tell what matter is like.

⬜ **Complete the chart.**

Thing	What color is it?	How does it feel?	How does it smell?

How Long Is It?

You can **measure** matter. You can use paper clips to measure how long something is.

You will need

- ★ 20 paper clips   ★ pencil   ★ crayon   ★ eraser
- ★ other things to measure

---

1. Join the paper clips.

2. Lay the clips on the table.

3. Lay your pencil beside the clips. Line up the end of the pencil with one end of the clips.

4. Count how many paper clips.

5. Write the number in the chart on the next page.

6. Measure other things.

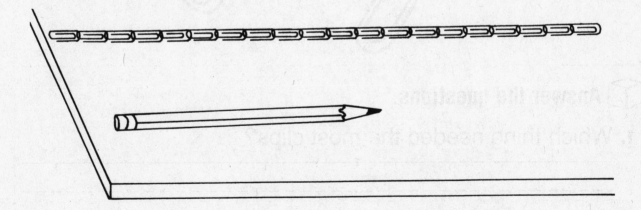

GO ON TO THE NEXT PAGE ☞

How Long Is It?, p. 2

 **Complete the chart.**

Things Measured	Number of Paper Clips
Pencil	

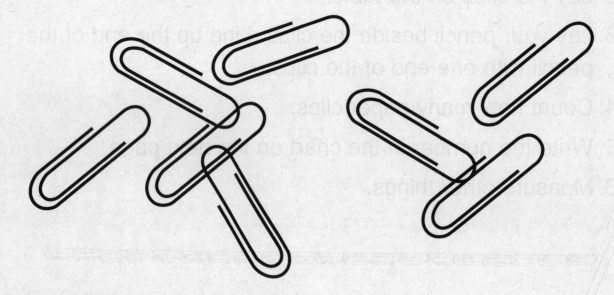

 **Answer the questions.**

1. Which thing needed the most clips?

_____

- -

_____

2. Which thing is the longest?

_____

- -

_____

How Much Does It Weigh?

You can measure matter. You can use a **scale** to measure how much something weighs.

You will need
- ⭐ kitchen scale
- ⭐ things to weigh (bottle of glue, book, etc.)
---

1. Choose one thing. Put it on the scale.

2. What number does the arrow on the scale point to?

3. Write the number in the chart on the next page.

4. Weigh other things.

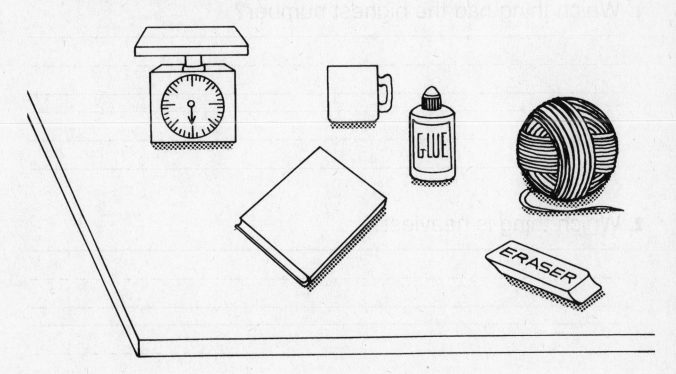

GO ON TO THE NEXT PAGE ☞

How Much Does It Weigh?, p. 2

 **Complete the chart.**

Things Weighed	Number Arrow Points To

 **Answer the questions.**

1. Which thing had the highest number?

_____

- -

_____

_____

- -

_____

2. Which thing is heaviest?

_____

- -

_____

_____

- -

_____

Kinds of Matter

Matter can be a **solid**, like wood. You can see a solid. It holds its **shape**. Matter can be a **liquid**, like water. You can see a liquid. It takes the shape of the container. Matter can be a **gas**, like air. Gas is usually invisible. It changes shape easily.

 **Color the solids in this picture red. Color the liquids in this picture blue. Do not color the gases.**

Solids

Matter can be a solid. You can see a solid. It holds its shape.

 **Circle the pictures of the solids. Color the pictures.**

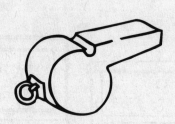

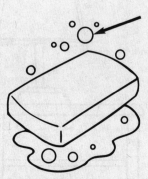

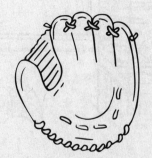

Liquids

Matter can be a liquid. You can see a liquid. It takes the shape of the container.

⬜ Circle the pictures of the liquids. Color the pictures.

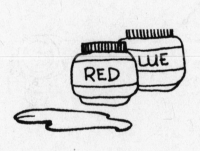  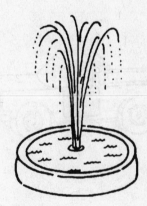

 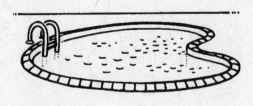 

Gases

Matter can be a gas. You usually cannot see a gas. It changes shape. It also can take the shape of the container.

 **Circle the pictures of the gases. Color the pictures.**

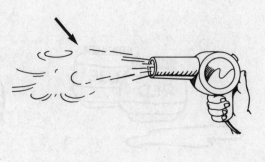

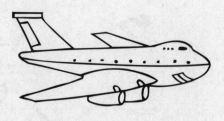

What Am I?

Use words from the box. Answer each question. Write the word on the line.

matter	solid	liquid	gas

1. I can be soft or hard.
I can be big or small.
I have a shape.
What am I?

_____

- - - - - - - - - - - - -

_____

2. I can pour.
My shape can change.
I am wet.
What am I?

_____

- - - - - - - - - - - - -

_____

3. You cannot see me.
I have no shape.
You can feel me when
I am wind.
What am I?

_____

- - - - - - - - - - - - -

_____

4. I am what things are
made of.
I have three forms.
What am I?

_____

- - - - - - - - - - - - -

_____

Can a Solid Change?

Solids keep their shape. Ice is a solid. Can ice change its shape?

You will need
- ☆ ice cubes   ☆ clock
- ☆ small self-sealing plastic bag

1. Place the ice cubes in the bag.

2. Put the bag in the sunlight.

3. Wait 30 minutes. What do you see?

Answer the questions.

1. What happened to the ice cubes?

_____

- -

_____

2. What made the ice melt?

_____

- -

_____

Can Water Change?

The **air** inside the room is warm. The warm air can change water.

You will need

★ pan   ★ water   ★ ruler

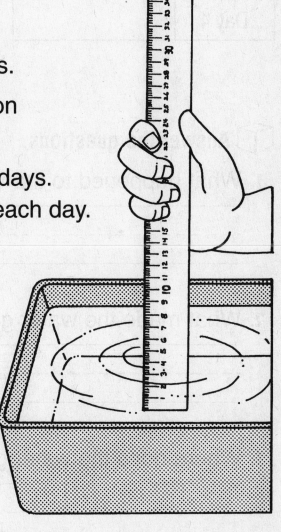

1. Fill the pan with water.
   Set the pan near a window.

2. Stand the ruler in the water.
   Measure how deep the water is.

3. Write the number in the chart on
   the next page.

4. Measure the water for 3 more days.
   Write the number in the chart each day.

GO ON TO THE NEXT PAGE ☞

Can Water Change?, p. 2

 **Complete the chart.**

Day	How Deep
Day 1	
Day 2	
Day 3	
Day 4	

Answer the questions.

1. What happened to the water?

   _____

   -

   _____

2. What made the water go away?

   _____

   -

   _____

3. Where does the water go?

   _____

   -

   _____

Does Air Change?

You know that solids and liquids can change. Does air change? Let's find out.

┌─ **You will need** ─────────────────────────────┐
│ ☆ clock   ★ 2 balloons   ☆ ruler   │
└──┘

1. Blow up 2 balloons.
   Make them the same size.

2. Measure the balloons from side to side.
   Fill in the chart on the next page.

3. Put one balloon where it is cold.
   Put one where it is hot.

4. Wait one hour.
   Get the 2 balloons.

5. Use the ruler.
   Measure the balloons from side to side.

GO ON TO THE NEXT PAGE ☞

Does Air Change?, p. 2

 Complete the chart.

Balloon	Measurement Before	Measurement After
Cold Balloon		
Hot Balloon		

 Answer the questions.

1. Did the balloons change? How?

_____

- -

_____

- -

_____

2. What does cold do to air?

_____

- -

_____

3. What does heat do to air?

_____

- -

_____

Push or Pull?

A **force** is a push or pull. You need force to move something.

 Write <u>push</u> or <u>pull</u> for each picture.

1. _____   **2.** _____

3. _____   **4.** _____

5. _____   **6.** _____

Pushes and Pulls

Things do not move on their own. It takes a force to move them. A force can start a thing moving. A force can change the direction that a thing is moving. A force can also make a thing stop moving.

A force is a push or pull. It takes a push to move a wheelbarrow. It takes a push to make an airplane fly. It takes a pull to move a wagon or a pull toy.

Color the toys you push. Circle the toy you pull.

Force Moves Things

You can move things by pushing or pulling. When you push or pull, you are using force.

┌─ **You will need** ─┐
★ 10 books
└────────────────────┘

1. Put one book on the table.

2. Push the book with one hand.
   Then, push the book with two hands.

3. Stack 10 books.

4. Push the books with one hand.
   Then, push the books with two hands.

GO ON TO THE NEXT PAGE 👉

Force Moves Things, p. 2

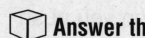 **Answer the questions.**

1. How many hands did it take to push one book?

_____

- -

_____

2. How many hands did it take to push 10 books?

_____

- -

_____

3. Was it harder to push one book or 10 books? Why?

_____

- -

_____

- -

_____

- -

_____

Which Is Easier to Move?

When you move something, two things rub together. The thing being moved rubs on the floor or table. The rubbing is called **friction**. The rubbing makes it harder to move something.

You will need

- ☆ block of wood
- ☆ rubber band
- ☆ string
- ☆ newspaper
- ☆ small pebbles

1. Put the rubber band around the block.
   Loop the string through the rubber band.

2. Put a piece of newspaper on a table, and put the block on the paper. Pull the string.

3. Put the pebbles on the newspaper.

4. Put the block on the pebbles.
   Pull the string.

GO ON TO THE NEXT PAGE ☞

Which Is Easier to Move?, p. 2

 Answer the questions.

1. Is the newspaper smooth or rough?

_____

- -

_____

2. Are the pebbles smooth or rough?

_____

- -

_____

3. Was it harder to pull the block over the newspaper or the pebbles? Why?

_____

- -

_____

- -

_____

- -

_____

Gentle Push, Hard Push

A gentle push will move a toy race car. But the car will go only a short distance. A hard push will make it go farther. The more force you use, the farther you can make something move.

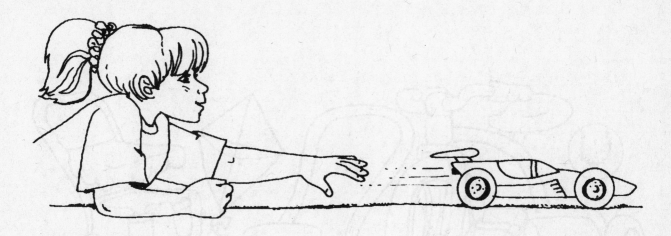

Answer the questions.

1. A gentle push will make a toy truck move a little bit. What kind of push will make it move a lot?

   _____

   –

   _____

2. What kind of push should you give a baby in a swing?

   _____

   –

   _____

Wheels Go Round

Some toys have **wheels** on them. Wheels make things easier to move. Wagons and wheelbarrows have wheels. Baby strollers and pull toys do, too.

Color the toys that have wheels on them.

The Force of Air

Air can move things. Moving air is called **wind**. Wind moves the clouds across the sky. Wind lifts your kite up high. Wind makes flags wave. Wind is a force because it moves things.

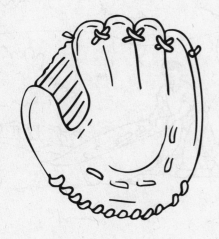 **Color the things that wind can move.**

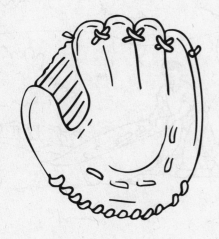

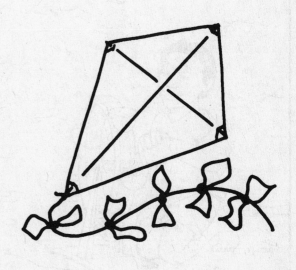

The Force of Water

Water can move things. Moving water makes a waterwheel turn. It pushes a boat down a river. It can even wash off muddy feet. Water is a force because it moves things.

Color the things the water can move.

Wind or Water?

Wind and water can move things. They are both forces. Sometimes, wind and water work together to move things.

☐ **Circle the force that moves each thing. Circle <u>wind</u> and <u>water</u> if both move the thing.**

1. 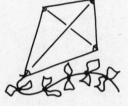   wind   water

2.    wind   water

3.    wind   water

4. 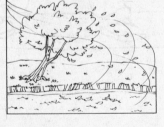   wind   water

5.    wind   water

Gravity

Gravity is a force that pulls everything toward the ground—plants, animals, buildings, and objects. Gravity keeps things on the Earth from floating off into space.

 **Lynnette and Tim will drop the blocks. Mark an X to show where each block will hit the ground.**

Gravity and Weight

Gravity pulls you toward the ground, too. Just step on a scale. See how much you weigh. Your **weight** is a measure of the pull of gravity on your body.

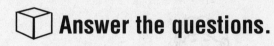 **Answer the questions.**

1. How much does Ei weigh?

_____

- - - - - - - -

_____ pounds

2. Ei and Jan are using a seesaw to see who weighs more. Which girl is heavier? Color her.

How Much Force?

It takes force to lift things because gravity pulls things down. It takes more force to lift some things than other things. Light things are easier to lift than heavy things. It takes more force to lift heavy things.

Circle the correct answer.

1. You need _____ to lift things.

  gravity   force

2. You need more force to lift _____ things.

  heavy   pull

3. Things that are easier to lift are_____.

  light   down

4. Things are pulled by _____.

  down   gravity

Which Takes More Force?

Which ones take more force to lift?

 **Look at the two things in each box. Which takes more force to lift? Color it.**

1.

2.

3.

4.

Puzzled About Force

 **Fill in the missing words. Write the words in the puzzle.**

Across

1. A force is a __ __ __ __ or a pull.

5. Moving __ __ __ __ __ can wash mud off your feet.

6. The pull of __ __ __ __ __ __ __ makes it easy to move down a slide.

Down

2. It is hard to lift __ __ __ __ __ things.

3. Wind is moving __ __ __.

4. It takes __ __ __ __ __ to lift things.

Magnets Have Force

Magnets have a special force. They pull things made of iron. This pull is called **attraction**.

You will need
- ☆ paper clip   ☆ rubber band   ☆ pencil   ☆ penny
- ☆ magnet   ☆ metal washer   ☆ comb   ☆ nail
---

1. Pick up the magnet.

2. Touch it to the paper clip.
   What do you see?

3. Fill in the chart on the next page.

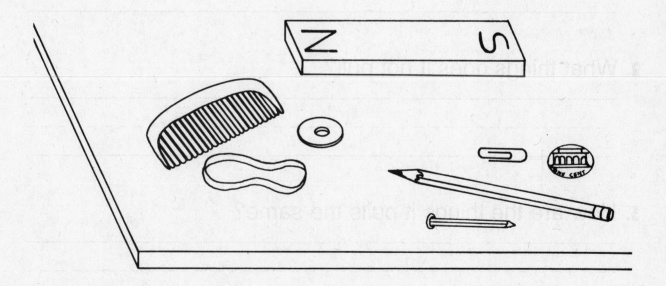

GO ON TO THE NEXT PAGE ☞

Magnets Have Force, p. 2

▢ Complete the chart.

Things a Magnet Pulls	Things a Magnet Does Not Pull

▢ Answer the questions.

1. What things does the magnet pull?

_____

- -

_____

2. What things does it not pull?

_____

- -

_____

3. How are the things it pulls the same?

_____

- -

_____

Poles Apart

The ends of a magnet are called **poles**. There is a north pole. It has an **N** on it. There is a south pole. It has an **S** on it.

Magnets can pull other magnets. Another word for pull is **attract**. Magnets can push other magnets, too. Another word for push is **repel**.

┌─ **You will need** ─────────┐
  ☆ 2 bar magnets
└────────────────────────────┘

1. Pick up one magnet.

2. Touch the S end to the N end of the other magnet.
   What happens?
   Fill in the chart on the next page.

3. Touch the S end to the S end of the other magnet.
   What happens?
   Fill in the chart on the next page.

4. Touch the N end to the S end of the other magnet.
   What happens?
   Fill in the chart on the next page.

5. Touch the N end to the N end of the other magnet.
   What happens?
   Fill in the chart on the next page.

GO ON TO THE NEXT PAGE ☞

Poles Apart, p. 2

 **Complete the chart.**

Poles	Push or Pull?
S and N	
S and S	
N and S	
N and N	

Answer the questions.

1. Which poles pull together?

_____

- -

2. Which poles push apart?

_____

- -

3. Do like poles pull together or push apart?

_____

- -

_____

- -

Which Magnet Parts Are the Strongest?

Magnets attract things made of iron. Each end of a magnet is called a pole. There is a pole marked **N**. It means North. There is pole marked **S**. It means South.

You will need ─────────────────────────────

☆ bar magnet   ☆ horseshoe magnet   ★ 20 paper clips

---

1. Have a friend hold the bar magnet.

2. Hang paper clips on the pole marked N.
   How many can you hang?
   Fill in the chart on the next page.

3. Hang paper clips on the pole marked S.
   How many can you hang?
   Fill in the chart on the next page.

4. Hang paper clips from the middle.
   How many can you hang?
   Fill in the chart on the next page.

5. Use the horseshoe magnet.
   Hang clips from each magnet part.
   Fill in the chart on the next page.

GO ON TO THE NEXT PAGE ☞

Which Magnet Parts Are the Strongest?, p. 2

◻ **Complete the chart.**

Magnet	Clips on N Pole	Clips on S Pole	Clips in Middle
Bar			
Horseshoe			

◻ **Answer the questions.**

1. Which parts of the magnet hold the most clips?

_____

_____

_____

2. Which parts of the magnet are strongest?

_____

_____

_____

Can You Make a Magnet?

A pull is a force. Magnets can pull things made of iron.
Magnets have a force.

You will need
- ✩ bar magnet
- ✩ iron nail
- ✩ 20 paper clips
---

1. Hold the magnet in one hand.
   Hold the nail in the other hand.

2. Rub the magnet across the nail 20 times.
   Be sure the magnet moves in the same way each time.

3. Try to pick up paper clips with the nail.
   What happens?

GO ON TO THE NEXT PAGE ☞

Can You Make a Magnet?, p. 2

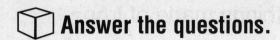 **Answer the questions.**

1. Can your new magnet pick up paper clips?

_____

- -

_____

2. How many clips can your magnet pick up?

_____

- -

_____

3. Is your new magnet strong?

_____

- -

_____

Taking Care of Magnets

Magnets have a force. Can they lose this force? Let's find out.

You will need

☆ bar magnet　　☆ iron nail　　☆ 20 paper clips

1. Make a magnet from a nail.
   See page 53.

2. Pick up paper clips.
   How many clips can you pick up?

3. Drop the nail on the floor 10 times.

4. Try to pick up paper clips.
   How many clips can you pick up?

GO ON TO THE NEXT PAGE ☞

Taking Care of Magnets, p. 2

 **Answer the questions.**

1. How many clips did the nail pick up before you dropped it?

_____

– –

_____

2. How many clips did the nail pick up after you dropped it?

_____

– –

_____

3. What happens when you drop a magnet?

_____

– –

_____

– –

_____

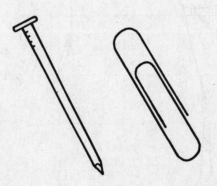

Electromagnets

A crane is a machine. It helps build tall buildings. It can lift big, heavy things. Some cranes use magnets. Electricity makes the magnet work. A person can turn the magnet on and off. When the electricity is on, the crane can lift things made of iron. When it is off, the magnet does not have any force. This kind of magnet is an **electromagnet**.

🔲 **Write a word to complete the sentences.**

1. Some _____ use magnets.

2. An _____ needs electricity to work.

3. When the electricity is off, the magnet does not have any _____.

Puzzled About Magnets

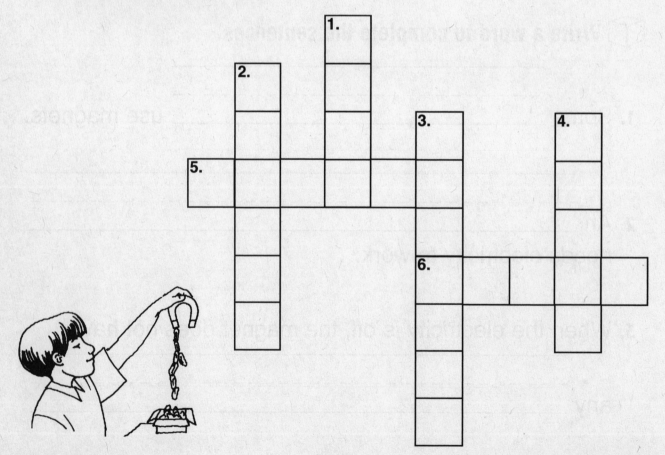 **Fill in the missing words. Write the words in the puzzle.**

| attract | magnet | iron | poles | cranes | repel |

Across

5. A __ __ __ __ __ __ picks up things made of iron.

6. To push apart means to __ __ __ __ __.

Down

1. A paper clip is made of __ __ __ __.

2. Some __ __ __ __ __ __ have electromagnets to lift big things.

3. To pull together means to __ __ __ __ __ __ __.

4. The ends of the magnet are called __ __ __ __ __.

Make a Compass

A **compass** is made with a magnet. A compass tells **direction**. It tells which way is north.

You will need

- ☆ compass
- ☆ magnet
- ☆ needle
- ☆ pan of water
- ☆ cork

---

1. Hold the magnet in one hand.
   Hold the needle in the other hand. Be careful.

2. Rub the magnet across the needle 20 times.
   Be sure the magnet moves in the same way each time.

3. Put the needle on the cork.

4. Put the cork in the water.

5. Spin the cork.

6. Look at the compass.
   Does the needle on the cork point north?

GO ON TO THE NEXT PAGE ☞

Make a Compass, p. 2

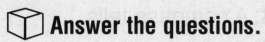 **Answer the questions.**

1. Did the needle point north?

_____

- -

_____

2. What makes the compass work?

_____

- -

_____

- -

_____

- -

Using Magnets

People use magnets in different ways. They use them for play and for work. They use them to pick things up, to hold things together, and to move things around.

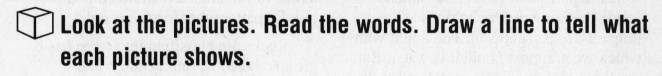 **Look at the pictures. Read the words. Draw a line to tell what each picture shows.**

1. 　　　　　　　　picks up things

2. 　　　　　　　　holds things together

3. 　　　　　　　　moves things around

Unit 2: Earth and Space Science

BACKGROUND INFORMATION

The Earth is made up of three materials: solids, liquids, and gases. The solids inside the Earth are such things as minerals, rocks, and soil. The liquid with which we are most familiar is water. But the Earth also has liquid metal and rock under its surface. And various gases, mostly oxygen and nitrogen, make up the atmosphere that allows life on the Earth.

The Earth
The Earth has a diameter of about 8,000 miles (12,900 km) and a circumference of about 25,000 miles (40,250 km). The Earth is made up of three layers. The outer layer of the Earth, called the crust, is quite thin, ranging from three to 34 miles (5–55 km) thick. We live on the crust, and most of the rocks and minerals we recognize come from the crust.

Below the crust is the mantle. The mantle is about 1,800 miles (2,900 km) thick, and it is made of mostly solid rock. The mantle is very hot, up to 5,400°F (3,000°C). Below the mantle is the core. The core is about 2,200 miles (3,500 km) thick, and it has a temperature as high as 7,200°F (4,000°C). Most scientists think the core has two parts, an outer core and an inner core. The outer core is made of melted iron and nickel. The inner core is a solid ball of iron and nickel.

Minerals and Rocks
Rocks are made up of minerals. Minerals have four characteristics that classify them as minerals. 1. They are substances that occur naturally. 2. They are inorganic solids. 3. Minerals of the same type usually have the same chemical composition. 4. The atoms of minerals are arranged in a regular pattern that forms crystals.

Rocks are classified into three basic groups: igneous, sedimentary, and metamorphic. These groups are based on how the rock is formed.

Igneous rocks begin as molten rock, a red-hot liquid. *Igneous* means "fire," so igneous rocks can be called "fire rocks." After a long while, the molten rock cools and hardens to form solid rock. The hardening can occur on the surface or below the surface of the Earth. Molten rock that is on the surface of the Earth is called lava. Granite is an example of igneous rock.

Sedimentary rocks are made up of sediments, or bits of rock and sand. The sediments piled up to form layers. The weight of the layers squeezed the sediments. Chemicals in the sediments cemented them together. The squeezing and cementing eventually caused the sediments to harden into layers of rock. Sandstone is an example of sedimentary rock.

Sometimes rocks that have already formed become buried deep in the Earth. There, great pressures inside the Earth squeeze the rocks. Great heat makes the rocks very hot but does not melt them. The squeezing and heat slowly change these rocks from one kind to another. The new kind of rock is called a metamorphic rock. *Metamorphic* means "changed." Igneous, sedimentary, and even other metamorphic rocks can be changed to form new metamorphic rocks. Slate is an example of metamorphic rock. Slate is formed from the sedimentary rock shale.

Soil

Soil is the grainy material that covers much of the land on the Earth. Soil is made of tiny bits of rock, minerals, organic materials, water, and air. Soil is needed for life to exist on the Earth. Plants need soil to grow. Then, animals, including people, eat the plants to stay alive.

Soil is created through a long process. Rocks break down through weathering and erosion into a stony product called parent soil. This type of soil is broken down further, mostly through weathering. Organic matter called humus mixes with the parent soil. When the long process is complete, the rock bits and humus have mixed to produce fertile soil, which is good for growing plants.

Weathering and Erosion

The Earth's surface undergoes constant change. Any process that causes rocks or landforms to break down is called weathering. Weathering is caused by several agents, including water, wind, ice, and plants. Weathering is usually a slow process, causing the gradual deterioration of the rocks or landforms.

Erosion is another way in which rocks and landforms are broken down or worn away. Erosion is the process in which weathered rock and soil are moved from one place to another. The most effective agents of erosion are moving water, waves, gravity, wind, and glaciers.

Fossils

A fossil is the preserved remains of a thing that was once alive, usually a plant or an animal. These remains are found in rock layers, so that if scientists know how old the rocks are, they can tell how old the plant or animal is. Scientists who study fossils are called paleontologists.

Most fossils form from a bone or a shell. Some fossils, though, mark the burrow or track of an animal; these are called trace fossils. Most fossils are found in sedimentary rock. But fossils have also been found in asphalt, frozen ice, and tree resin.

Water

Water is our most precious resource. Water covers about 70 percent of the Earth's surface. Without water, life could not exist. Our bodies are about 65 percent water. We use water in many ways. Water is an amazing substance, too. It can be a solid, a liquid, and a gas. It can change from a solid state (ice) to a liquid state (water) to a gaseous state (water vapor) and back again.

The Water Cycle

Water often changes from its liquid form to its gaseous form and back to its liquid form in a process called the water cycle. The three main steps in the water cycle are evaporation, condensation, and precipitation. Evaporation is necessary to get the liquid water into its gaseous form of water vapor in the air. Condensation is needed to turn the vapor back to a liquid in the clouds. And precipitation returns the liquid water to the Earth.

Evaporation occurs as liquid water is heated and changed into water vapor. The water vapor is then carried up into the sky by rising air. Condensation takes place as the rising water vapor cools and is changed into liquid water, forming clouds. Precipitation happens as water droplets grow heavy and fall to the Earth as rain, snow, or some other type of precipitation.

Gases and the Atmosphere

We live on the crust of the Earth. We have food and water. But another part of the Earth's structure is necessary to sustain life.

That part is called the atmosphere. The atmosphere is made up of various gases, mostly nitrogen and oxygen, that allow us to survive on the Earth. The atmosphere is about 500 miles (800 km) high, and it is held in place by the Earth's gravity.

The atmosphere has four layers. Closest to the Earth is the troposphere, the layer in which we live. The troposphere is only a thin band, about five to ten miles (8–16 km) thick. All the Earth's weather occurs in the troposphere. The troposphere also contains the air we need to live. The air in the troposphere is about 80 percent nitrogen and 20 percent oxygen. There are also small amounts of other gases, including argon and carbon dioxide.

Above the troposphere is the stratosphere, a layer that is from about five to 50 miles (8–80 km) high. The stratosphere has only a few clouds, which are mostly made of ice crystals. In the stratosphere are the fast-moving winds known as the jet stream. The air in the lower part of the stratosphere is cold. In the upper part of the stratosphere, the temperature increases. The important ozone layer is in the upper stratosphere. The ozone absorbs ultraviolet energy from the Sun, which causes the temperature there to rise. The ozone layer is important because it protects creatures on the Earth from the harmful ultraviolet rays.

Above the stratosphere is the ionosphere, which stretches from about 50 miles to about 300 miles (80–500 km) above the Earth. There is almost no air in the ionosphere. But the ionosphere is useful for radio astronomy and communication with satellites. The natural displays of light called auroras occur in the ionosphere.

The top layer of the atmosphere is called the exosphere. It begins about 300 miles (500 km) above the Earth, but it has no definite top boundary. This layer is the beginning of what we call outer space. The exosphere contains mostly oxygen and helium gases. This layer also has a very high temperature, up to several thousand degrees.

Weather

Weather, in its most basic explanation, is caused by the uneven heating of the Earth's surface by the Sun. The land and the water are heated differently. This uneven heating causes pockets of air with different temperatures. Cool air is heavier than warm air. As a result, the cooler air moves under the warmer air, so the lighter warm air is pushed up. This movement of air causes winds. These factors all work together to produce weather.

We live in the layer of the Earth's atmosphere called the troposphere. Air in the troposphere moves constantly. The air is heated, not directly by the Sun, but by the air's contact with the Earth. Air closer to the Earth is warmer than air higher up. Cold air is heavier than warm air, so the cold air moves downward. The warm air rises as it is displaced, setting up the patterns of air circulation in the troposphere.

Near the Earth's surface, the sinking air results in high-pressure zones called ridges. The rising air creates low-pressure zones called troughs. The differences in air pressure produce winds. Wind moves out of high-pressure zones in a clockwise direction and into low-pressure zones in a counterclockwise direction. Weather data identifies winds by the direction from which they come. For example, a wind moving toward the south is called a north wind, because north is the direction from which it comes.

Great air masses move slowly across the Earth's surface. These moving air masses take on the characteristics of the surface beneath them. Air moving over a warm surface is warmed, and air moving over a cold surface is cooled. Air moving over water becomes moist, and air moving over land becomes drier. As it moves, the air mass causes changes in the weather of an area.

Wind

Wind is a good source of energy. Wind currents are the result of uneven heating of the Earth's surface by the Sun. Wind has the energy to move leaves, trees, and in cases of storms, houses. Windmills have been used for hundreds of years to use the wind's energy. Just like water, wind was used to grind grain. People also used windmills to pump water. Wind energy can also be transferred into electric energy.

Fronts

A front is a line or boundary between air masses. The air masses clash along the front, so weather along a front is often stormy. A cold front occurs when a cold air mass replaces a warm air mass. Weather along a cold front often includes thunderstorms with much precipitation. A warm front occurs when a warm air mass replaces a cold air mass. Precipitation may also occur along a warm front, but the precipitation is usually not as heavy as along a cold front. A stationary front occurs when air masses meet without moving. A stationary front may produce an extended period of precipitation.

Precipitation

Precipitation is one of the most obvious features of weather. As you recall, precipitation is the third step in the water cycle, following evaporation and condensation. Sometimes precipitation does not fall in an area for a long period of time. Plants and crops can die, and sometimes even animals and people die as a result of the lack of water. When an area does not receive precipitation for a long time, it is said to be in a drought.

Clouds

Another of the most obvious, and sometimes most spectacular, features of weather is the cloud. Clouds can take several forms, from thin and wispy to dense and billowy. How do clouds form? Remember the movement of air, with warm air rising as the cold air sinks? First, through evaporation, water on the Earth's surface becomes water vapor in the air. As the warm air rises and expands, it naturally begins to cool. Water vapor in the air starts to condense around tiny particles in the air, such as dust or smoke, forming droplets. Clouds form in different shapes, depending on their height, the coolness of the air, and the amount of water vapor in the air.

The water droplets grow bigger as more water vapor condenses. When the droplets get so large they cannot be held up by the rising air, they fall as rain or some other form of precipitation. If the cloud is cold and contains crystals of ice, snow may fall instead of rain.

There are three main types of clouds: cirrus, cumulus, and stratus. Cirrus clouds are high above the Earth and are usually seen in fair weather. These clouds, made of ice crystals, are wispy and streak the sky. Cumulus clouds are white and fluffy, looking much like cotton balls. They are often seen in good weather, though they can produce rain showers or snow. Stratus clouds are low, dark clouds close to the Earth. They often produce rain or snow.

Stormy Weather

Weather comes in many forms, fair and foul. Fair weather includes sunny days, gentle breezes, and mild temperatures. But foul weather is more spectacular, accompanied as it often is by powerful displays of wind, rain, lightning, and thunder. One of the most common examples of foul weather is the thunderstorm. Approaching thunderstorms are often accompanied by towering cumulus clouds called thunderheads. These billowy clouds have flat tops and dark bottoms. Thunderheads are formed when warm, moist air rises. As the rising air begins to cool, water vapor in the air condenses, and cumulus clouds form. The hot ground causes the heated air to rise faster and higher. The cumulus clouds grow larger and taller, often reaching ten miles or more (16 km or more) into the air. As the clouds grow in size, they become more likely to produce rain.

Thunderheads also produce two well-known features of stormy weather: lightning and thunder. Lightning is an electrical spark caused by friction inside the thunderhead. As the clouds grow, raindrops scrape against each other, and friction is produced. This friction builds up an electrical charge, just as you do when you scrape your feet across a carpet. Most of the electric charges in the lower part of the cloud are negative. These negative charges emit a spark that jumps toward a positive charge on the ground. This spark is what we call lightning. The lightning instantly heats the air around its path. This heated air expands quickly and collides with cooler air. The collision between the heated air and the cooler air produces the sound we know as thunder.

The Sun
Life on the Earth begins with the Sun, and the Earth's weather is also caused by the Sun and its energy. The Sun produces energy in the form of heat and light. In the center of the Sun, its core, nuclear fusion reactions change hydrogen into helium. These reactions release an unbelievable amount of energy. At the core, the Sun burns at a temperature of about 27 million degrees F (15 million degrees C). The energy moves from the core to the surface of the Sun, which has a temperature of almost 4 million degrees F (2.2 million degrees C). The energy then travels

through space as electromagnetic waves of light and heat.

The Earth is 93 million miles (150 million km) from the Sun, so only a tiny amount of the Sun's energy reaches the Earth. But this small amount is enough to sustain life and create weather on the Earth. Much of the Sun's energy and harmful rays are filtered out by the Earth's atmosphere. About half of the Sun's energy is absorbed or reflected by the ozone, clouds, or the air. About 50 percent is absorbed by the Earth's surface.

The Sun is much larger than the Earth, with a diameter of about 840,000 miles (1,352,000 km), compared to the Earth's diameter of about 8,000 miles (12,900 km). But the Sun is, in fact, only a medium-sized star. Many early people believed that the Sun moved around the Earth, but the opposite is true. The Earth orbits around the Sun, once every 365 days or 1 year.

The Solar System
The Earth joins eight other planets in the solar system. These nine planets orbit around the Sun. (Recent research by astronomers suggests there may be a tenth planet somewhere beyond Pluto.) They all receive energy from the Sun, but they receive varying amounts based on their distance from the Sun. The inner planets (Mercury, Venus, Earth, Mars) receive more energy because they are closer. The outer planets (Jupiter, Saturn, Uranus, Neptune, Pluto) are very cold planets where the chance of life is very small. Students can remember the order of the planets outward from the Sun by using this saying: "My Very Energetic Mother Just Sent Us Nine Pizzas."

The other planets are mostly quite different from the Earth. The planet closest to the Sun, Mercury, has a year, or one orbit of the Sun, that is only 88 Earth days long. On Mercury, the surface temperature can be as low as about –290°F (–173°C) or as high as 800°F (425°C). For the most distant planet, Pluto, one orbit takes 248 Earth years. Pluto is about three billion miles (4.8 billion km) from the Sun. On Neptune, winds sometimes blow up to 700 miles per hour (1,125 km per hour).

The planets are held in their orbits by the Sun's gravitational pull. Likewise, the Earth and the farther planets have smaller bodies, or moons, that orbit around them, held by each planet's gravitational pull. The Earth has one moon. On the other hand, Jupiter has at least 17 moons.

The Moon

The Moon is a satellite of the Earth. It is about one fourth the size of the Earth, with a diameter of about 2,100 miles (3,400 km). The Moon appears about the same size as the Sun in the sky, but that is only because the Moon is so much closer than the Sun. The Moon is about 240,000 miles (384,000 km) from the Earth, and the Sun is about 93 million miles (150 million km). The Moon orbits the Earth once about every 29 days.

The Moon has no light of its own, but it seems to shine because it reflects the Sun's light. The Moon also has no atmosphere and no life. The Moon's gravity is only about one sixth as strong as the Earth's gravity. A person who weighs 60 pounds (27 kg) on the Earth would weigh only 10 pounds (4.5 kg) on the Moon!

Phases of the Moon

The Moon revolves around the Earth, causing the Moon's phases. The Moon has no light of its own; it only reflects the Sun's light. This reflected light is visible from the Earth in different amounts during periods called phases. When the Moon is between the Sun and the Earth, only the Moon's side away from the Earth is lit.

The side facing the Earth is unlit; this phase is called the New Moon.

A little more of the Moon becomes visible each day after the New Moon phase. At first, a small crescent of light appears on the Moon's eastern edge; this is called a crescent Moon. This crescent grows larger each day. A week after the New Moon phase, half of the Moon facing the Earth is lighted; this phase is called the First Quarter. After another week, the Earth is between the Sun and the Moon; all of the Moon facing the Earth is lighted. This phase is called the Full Moon. Though the phase is called the Full Moon, the Moon is only truly fully lighted on one night. Between the New Moon and Full Moon phases, the Moon is said to be waxing.

A week after the Full Moon phase, only half of the Moon facing the Earth is lighted. This phase is called the Last Quarter. Another week later, the Moon returns to the New Moon phase. Between the Full Moon phase and the return to the New Moon phase, the Moon is said to be waning.

The complete cycle of phases for the Moon takes about 29.5 days. The phases are caused by the Moon's changing position in relation to the Earth and the Sun. Because the Earth blocks sunlight from reaching parts of the Moon, only those lighted parts of the Moon are visible from the Earth.

Stars

Stars are great balls of gas that burn at tremendous temperatures. Our Sun is the nearest star. Most stars are very, very far away. Stars are very, very bright, but they seem dim to us because of their great distance, like a burning match many miles away. Stars differ from one another in their color, brightness, and size. One of the brighter stars seen from the Earth is Polaris, also known as the North Star.

Some stars appear grouped in recognizable shapes. These groups are called constellations. Most constellations were named by ancient people. Some constellations are Orion, Leo, Scorpius, and Ursa Major, also called the Great Bear. The Big Dipper is part of Ursa Major. Constellations are noted on star charts, which are like maps of the sky. On a clear night, about 6,000 stars are visible to the unaided eye.

A larger grouping of stars is called a galaxy. Galaxies contain billions of stars, and there are billions of galaxies in the universe. Our solar system is in the Milky Way galaxy. On a clear, dark night, away from city lights, the Milky Way is visible as a sparkling band across the sky.

Studying the Skies

A place that gives shows about the stars and planets is called a planetarium. You can make a simple planetarium with a flashlight and an oatmeal box or frozen juice can. Carefully punch the shape of a constellation in the end of the box or can. Then, in a dark room, shine the flashlight inside the box or can and project the constellation on the wall or ceiling.

RELATED READING

- *Cloud Dance* by Thomas Locker (Harcourt, 2000).

- *Cloudy Day, Sunny Day* by Donald Crews (Green Light Readers, 1999).

- *Compost! Growing Gardens from Your Garbage* by Linda Glaser (Millbrook, 1996).

- *A Handful of Dirt* by Raymond Bial (Walker & Company, 2000).

- *The Man in the Moon* by Christine Price (Steck-Vaughn, 1997).

- *Our Big Home: An Earth Poem* by Linda Glaser (Millbrook, 2000).

- *A Pocketful of Stars: Poems About the Night* compiled by Nikki Siegen-Smith (Barefoot Books, 1999).

- *Snow* by Uri Shulevitz (Farrar, Straus & Giroux, 1998).

- *Starry Messenger* by Peter Sis (Farrar, Straus & Giroux, 1996).

- *Water Dance* by Thomas Locker (Harcourt Brace, 1997).

- *We Like the Sun* by Ena Keo (Steck-Vaughn, 1997).

Unit 2 Assessment

⬡ **Read each sentence. Circle _true_ or _false_.**

1. Water can change rocks.   true   false

2. Rocks can break down into small pieces.   true   false

3. A fossil is made of wood.   true   false

4. Rain comes from clouds.   true   false

5. Clouds are made of stones.   true   false

6. Weather can change.   true   false

7. The Moon is bigger than the Sun.   true   false

8. The Sun is a star.   true   false

GO ON TO THE NEXT PAGE ☞

Unit 2 Assessment, p. 2

⬛ **Which word makes the sentence true? Circle it. Then, write the word in the sentence.**

9. Rocks break down to make _____.

    wind   rain   sand

10. Wind and _____ can change the Earth.

    thermometers   water   wood

11. Thermometers measure _____.

    wind   clouds   temperature

12. The Earth _____ all the time.

    turns   falls   rains

13. The Sun gives us _____.

    night   gold   day

Rocks

© Steck-Vaughn Company

Rocks are different from each other in many ways. They are different colors, different sizes, and different shapes. Some are rough, and some are smooth. Some are harder than others.

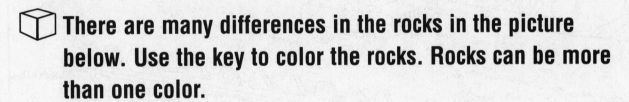 **There are many differences in the rocks in the picture below. Use the key to color the rocks. Rocks can be more than one color.**

Key:
large rocks = yellow
small rocks = blue
smooth rocks = red
rough rocks = green

How Are Rocks Used?

📦 Color all the rocks and the things made of rocks.

How Hard Are Rocks?

Are some rocks harder than others? Let's find out.

You will need

★ 3 or 4 different kinds of rocks (including chalk)

★ nail

★ safety goggles

Safety First

Since the students often put their faces very close to what they are doing and a nail could slip, have them wear safety goggles.

1. Scratch each rock with a nail.

2. Put the soft rocks in one pile.

3. Put the hard rocks in another pile.

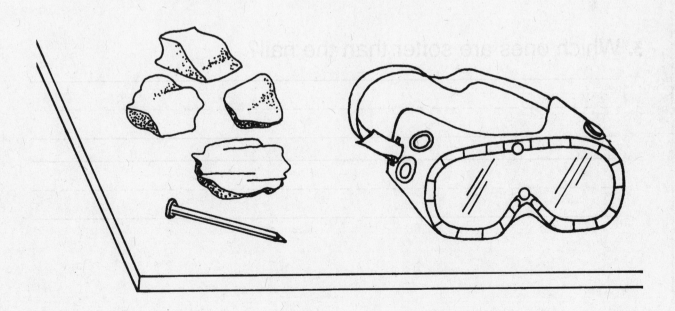

GO ON TO THE NEXT PAGE ☞

How Hard Are Rocks?, p. 2

Answer the questions.

1. What happened to each rock?

_____

- -

_____

_____

2. Which rocks are harder than the nail?

_____

- -

_____

_____

3. Which ones are softer than the nail?

_____

- -

_____

_____

Can Water Change Rocks?

You know that some rocks are hard. Some rocks are soft. Can water change rocks? Let's find out.

1. Put some soft rocks, like sandstone, in a jar.

2. Add some water. Put on the lid.

3. Shake the jar many times. Shake it for a half hour.

4. Look at the rocks. Did they change?

_____

- -

_____

- -

_____

Soil in the Garden

Soil is part of a garden. Soil holds the plants. It also holds the water and nutrients that plants need. When we look at soil, we might see just brown or tan dirt. But if we observe soil more closely, we can see many other things.

Draw a picture of how you think the soil looks underground.

What Is in Soil?

Rocks are one thing in soil. Rocks split into smaller and smaller pieces until they become **pebbles**, then **sand**, and then **dust**. These things become part of the soil.

Parts of animals are also in soil. When the animals die, they break down into tiny pieces. There are pieces of **bones**, **feathers**, and **shells**. There are also dead **insects** and **worms**.

Another part of soil is dead plants. If you look at soil, you will probably see pieces of **leaves**, **roots**, and **wood**. You might also see **petals** from flowers.

Look at the paragraphs above. Use the words in dark print to finish the chart.

WHAT IS IN SOIL?

Rock Parts	Animal Parts	Plant Parts
1.	1.	1.
2.	2.	2.
3.	3.	3.
	4.	4.
	5.	

What Else Is in Soil?

There are little holes in the soil underground. The holes are filled with air. The air spaces give a plant's roots room to grow.

There is another reason for the holes underground. When it rains, the holes fill with water. The water mixes with **nutrients** in the soil. Then, the roots of plants take the water and the nutrients from the soil. The water and the nutrients go into the plants.

Draw another picture of how you think the soil looks underground. Compare this picture to the one you made on page 76.

Types of Soils

There are many kinds of soils. Each kind looks different and feels different from other kinds.

Sandy soil is very loose. The grains of **sand** can be seen easily.

Clay soil holds together well. Grains of clay are very small. Some are too small to be seen.

Potting soil is sand and clay. It is loose but still holds together. The grains can be seen easily.

Draw lines to match the words with the kinds of soil.

1. large grains   clay

2. small grains   sand

3. mixed grains   potting soil

Soils for Planting

Plants that grow well in one kind of soil may not grow well in another. That is why people who plant gardens use special kinds of soil when they plant.

Clay holds a lot of water, but it gets hard. Roots can't grow well in it. The roots of a plant can spread out in sandy soil. But sand doesn't hold water well. Potting soil is clay and sand mixed together.

☐ **Would plants grow well in potting soil? On another sheet of paper, tell why or why not.**

Tiny Rocks in Soil

If you looked at sand through a hand lens, you would see that sand is really tiny rocks. Over hundreds of years, big rocks break down to make sand. You would also see that sand is different colors.

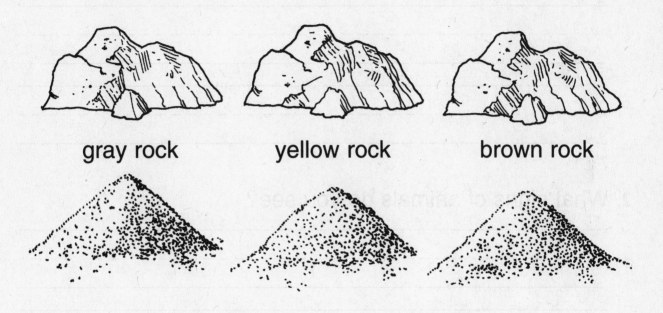

gray rock   yellow rock   brown rock

📦 **Color the rocks above. Then, color the sand from the rocks. Why is sand different colors?**

_____

- -

_____

- -

_____

- -

_____

Animals in the Soil

What kinds of animals live in soil?

Take a walk near your home. Look at the soil. Answer the questions.

1. What animals are in the soil?

_____

- -

_____

- -

_____

2. What signs of animals do you see?

_____

- -

_____

- -

_____

Dinosaur Times

Dinosaurs lived on the Earth long, long ago. They lived before there were people on the Earth. The dinosaurs died out long ago.

⬛ **Answer the questions.**

1. Where did dinosaurs live?

_____

_____

2. When did dinosaurs live?

_____

_____

3. Did people ever see a living dinosaur?

_____

_____

4. What happened to the dinosaurs?

_____

_____

Fossils from Long Ago

We know about animals that lived long ago by fossils that are found. **Fossils** are pieces of stone that show us how plants and animals looked.

Some animals became stuck in tar pools and died. Scientists found their bones. Scientists put their bones together to see what the animals looked like.

Match each word to the sentence.
Write the letter of your answer on the line.

_____ 1. fossils

_____ 2. tar pools

_____ 3. bones

a. Scientists put these together to see how animals looked.

b. These are pieces of stone.

c. Animals got stuck here and died.

Fossil Bones

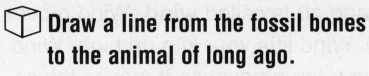 **Draw a line from the fossil bones to the animal of long ago.**

1.

a.

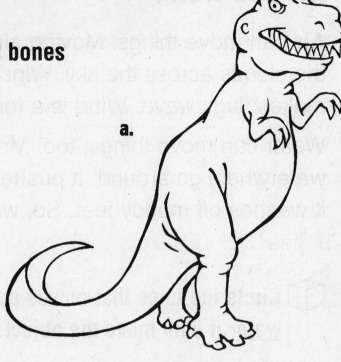

2.

b.

3.

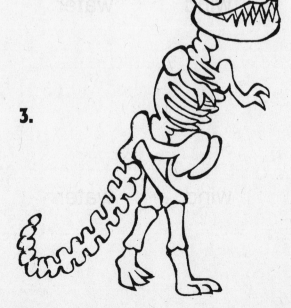

c.

Air and Water

Air can move things. Moving air is called **wind**. Wind moves the clouds across the sky. Wind lifts your kite up high. Wind makes flags wave. Wind is a force because it moves things.

Water can move things, too. Moving water makes a waterwheel go around. It pushes a boat down a stream. And it washes off muddy feet. So, water is also a force.

▢ Circle the force that moves each object. Circle <u>wind</u> and <u>water</u> if both move the object.

1. 　　　　　　　wind　　　water

2. 　　　　　　　wind　　　water

3. 　　　　　　　wind　　　water

Gone with the Wind!

Ready. Set. Go! The sailboat race has begun. Two boats are in the race. They are almost alike. But one of them has larger **sails**. Which sailboat do you think will win?

Boats have used sails for many years. Sails catch the wind. A large sail catches more wind than a small one. The force of the wind pushes against a sail. This force makes the boat travel across the water.

📦 Answer the questions.

1. Color the picture of the sailboat you think will win.
2. Complete this sentence.
   The sailboat I colored will win because it has

   _____

   -

   _____.

Using Air

Look at the picture. Circle the things that use air. Color the picture.

Air Is Real

☐ **Finish each sentence. Write your answer on the line.**

1. The children can _____ the air.

see   feel

2. Moving air is called _____.

wind   Sun

3. Moving air feels _____.

warm   cool

4. The air in the woods is _____.

dirty   clean

5. The animals _____ the air.

breathe   drink

Air and Weather

Air has a lot to do with **weather**.

 **Cut out the sentences at the bottom of the page. Paste each one under the correct picture.**

✂

It is a wet day.	The air feels cool.
The air feels warm.	It is not windy.
The wind is blowing.	It is a dry day.

How Are Clouds Made?

You have seen **clouds** in the sky. How are clouds made?

📦 **Show a way clouds are made. Cut out the pictures at the bottom of the page. Paste them in the squares.**

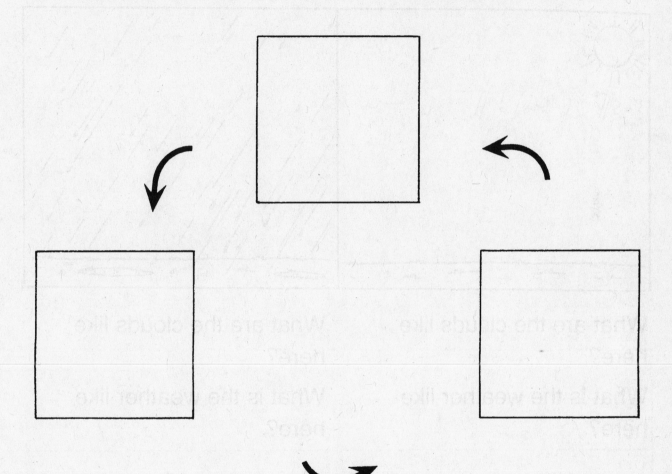

Clouds and Weather

Clouds can tell you about the weather.

☐ **Cut out the pictures at the bottom of the page. Paste each one in the correct box. Color the pictures.**

What are the clouds like here?

What is the weather like here?

What are the clouds like here?

What is the weather like here?

All About Clouds

What do you know about clouds?

◻ **Circle the correct answer.**

1. Rain comes from _____.

   clothes   clouds   louds

2. Clouds are made of tiny drops of _____.

   water   later   waiter

3. Clouds look _____ when it rains.

   bark   drank   dark

4. Clouds look _____ in the Sun.

   wait   tight   white

5. Weather can _____.

   chain   change   chin

Reading the Thermometer

A **thermometer** tells how hot or cold it is.

 Look at each picture. Look at each thermometer. Write <u>warm</u> or <u>cold</u> on each line. Color the pictures.

1.

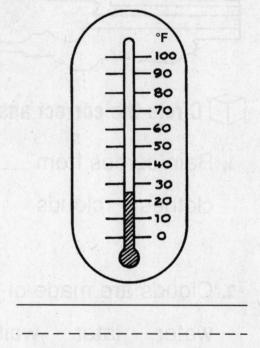

_____

- - - - - - - - - - - - - - - -

_____

2.

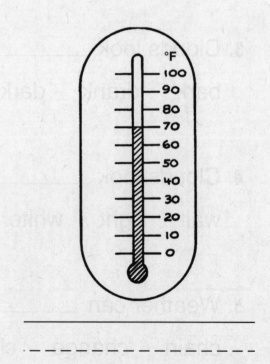

_____

- - - - - - - - - - - - - - - -

_____

Measuring Temperature

Use a thermometer to measure **temperature**.

1. Measure the air temperature in the four places shown above the thermometers.

2. Color each picture. Show how the thermometer looked.

3. Write the temperature of each place.

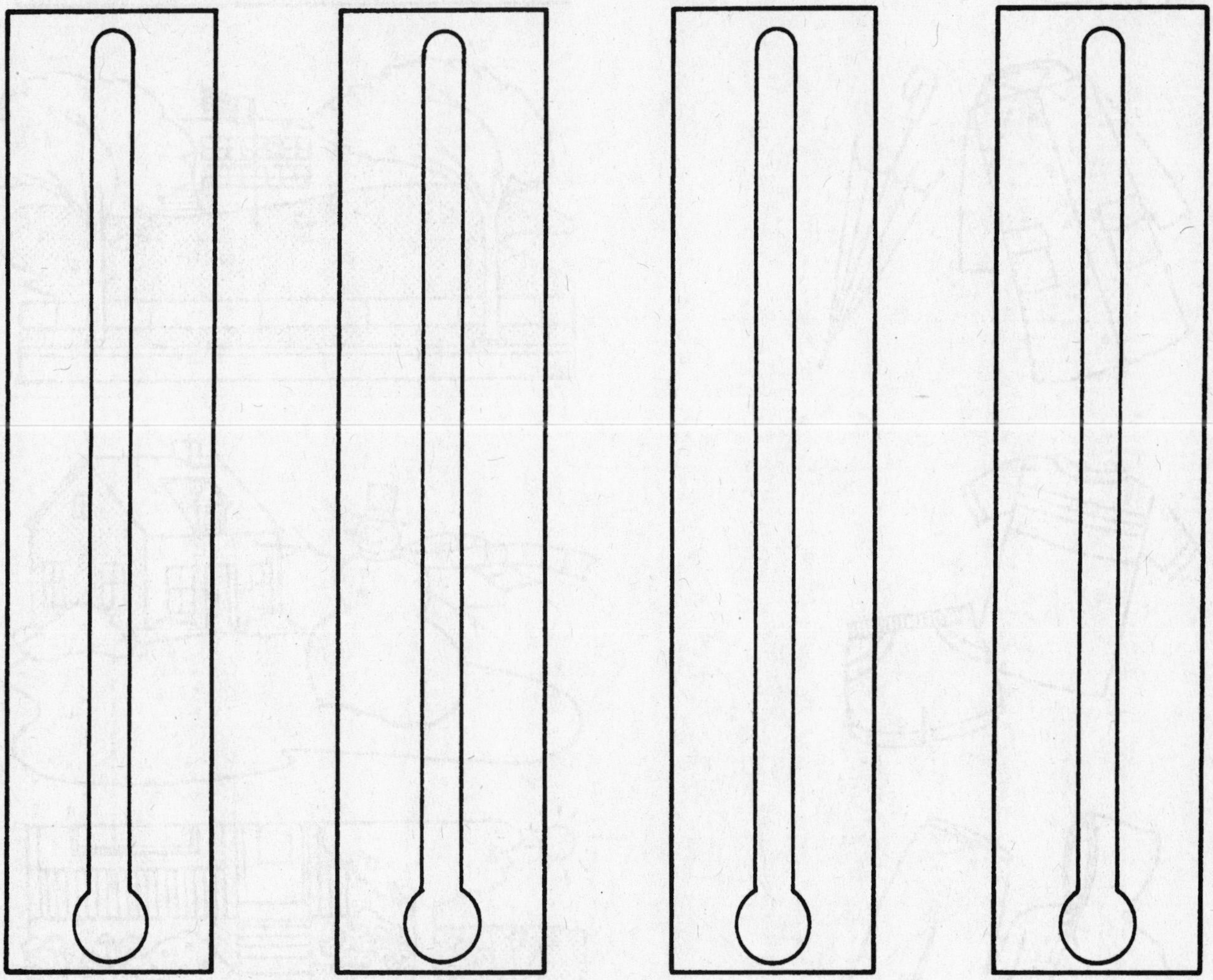

On the floor	Window ledge	Near the ceiling	Outside

_____ °C   _____ °C   _____ °C   _____ °C

_____ °F   _____ °F   _____ °F   _____ °F

Dress for the Weather

How would you dress for the weather?

📦 **Draw lines to match the clothes with the weather.**

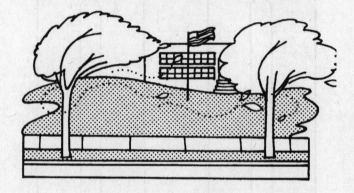

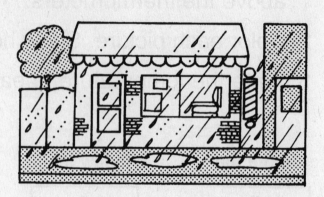

What Will the Weather Be?

Predict means to guess. Can you predict the weather?

You will need

☆ construction paper ☆ crayons

☆ thumbtacks or tape ☆ scissors
---

1. Draw pictures to show different kinds of weather (sunny, cloudy, rainy, snowy). Make a big chart like the one below.

2. Today, guess what the weather will be like tomorrow. Put a picture of it on the chart. Make the chart for five days of the week.

3. Tomorrow, put a picture under your guess to show what the weather was really like.

4. Do this each day for five days.

Our Weather				
Monday	Tuesday	Wednesday	Thursday	Friday
we think	we think			

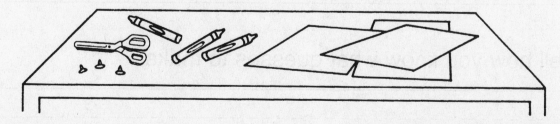

GO ON TO THE NEXT PAGE ☞

What Will the Weather Be?, p. 2

◻ **Complete the chart.**

OUR WEATHER

	Monday	Tuesday	Wednesday	Thursday	Friday
We Predict					
What the Weather Is					

◻ **Answer the questions.**

1. Did the weather change?

_____

- -

_____

2. Did you make good guesses?

_____

- -

_____

3. Tell how you know what guesses to make.

_____

- -

_____

The Sun

The **Sun** is a **star**. It is not the biggest star. And it is not the brightest star. It looks big and bright because it is the closest star to us. It is close enough for us to feel its heat.

Like other stars, the Sun is a ball of hot gases. Light and heat from the Sun come to the Earth. Nothing could live on the Earth without the light and heat of the Sun.

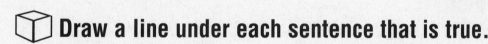 **Draw a line under each sentence that is true.**

1. The Sun is a star.

2. The Sun is a ball of hot gases.

3. The Sun is the biggest and brightest star.

4. We get heat and light from the Sun.

Around We Go!

The Earth moves around the Sun in a path. Its path is called an **orbit**. The Earth moves once around the Sun each year. It always travels along the same orbit.

🔲 **Draw a line to show the path the Earth follows around the Sun.**

🔲 **Complete the sentences.**

1. The Earth's path around the Sun is called an

_____

_____ .

2. The Earth goes around the Sun once each

_____

_____ .

What Makes Day and Night?

The Earth orbits the Sun. The Earth also moves in another way. Once every day, it slowly turns around. This turning of the Earth is called **rotation**. The rotation of the Earth gives us day and night.

It is day when the place you live is facing the Sun. It is night when the place you live is facing away from the Sun.

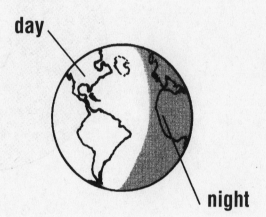

day

night

 **Circle the missing word or words.**

1. The Earth turns around once each _____.

    day   week   month   year

2. The Earth's rotation gives us _____.

    snow and rain   day and night

Light from the Sun

We get **light** from the Sun.

 **Where should the Sun be? Draw it.**

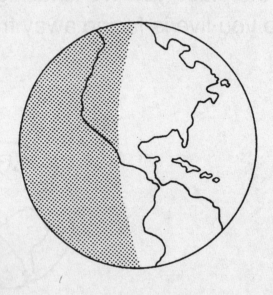

 **Where is it night on Earth? Color that part.**

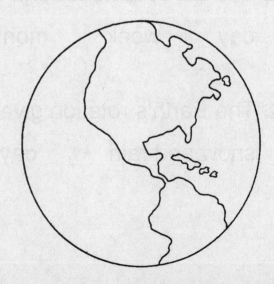

Light and Heat

The Sun gives us light and heat. We get light and heat from other things, too.

⬜ **Circle the things that give us light or heat. Then, color the pictures.**

Which Will Dry Faster?

The Sun and the clouds bring changes.

📦 **In which picture will the clothes dry faster? Color the one that will dry faster.**

Sun and Earth Facts

How much do you know about the Sun and the Earth?

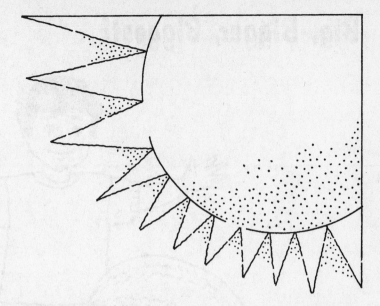

 Circle the correct word. Then, write the word in the sentence.

1. The Sun gives us _____.

flight   light   right

2. The Sun shines on the _____.

Earth   hearth   birth

3. The Sun gives us _____.

bay   hay   day

4. The Earth _____.

urns   turns   burns

Big, Bigger, Biggest!

big   **bigger**   **biggest**

Tito made a model. A **model** shows what something is like. Tito's model is of the Earth, the Moon, and the Sun. He wanted to show that the Moon is big, the Earth is bigger, and the Sun is biggest of all.

Tito used a peanut for the Moon. He used an orange for the Earth. And he used a watermelon for the Sun. Tito hopes his class can learn something from his model.

Look at the picture above. Help Tito complete his model. Draw a line to show which word belongs with each food.

The Earth Turns

Shadows change because the Earth keeps turning. You can watch a shadow change.

 On a sunny day, put a stick in the ground. Draw where the shadow is at each time of day.

1. Morning (10:00)

2. Lunch (12:00)

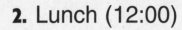

3. Afternoon (1:30)

4. Later Afternoon (3:00)

Shine On!

Sun

Moon

The Sun is a star. Like other stars, the Sun makes its own light. The Sun's light comes from gases burning in the Sun.

There are no gases burning in the **Moon**, because the Moon is not a star. So, the Moon does not make light.

Why, then, does the Moon look bright at night? It looks bright because the Sun's light is shining on it. The Moon looks bright because it **reflects** the Sun's light. In this way, the Moon is like a mirror.

Circle each line that tells about the Moon.

1. a burning ball of gases

2. does <u>not</u> make its own light

3. reflects the Sun's light

How Does the Moon Seem to Change?

The Moon seems to change its shape. Each different way the Moon looks is called a **phase**.

Use a yellow crayon to color the part of the Moon we can see from the Earth. Color the sky black.

MOON PHASES

Sometimes the Moon looks as round as a ball. It shines brightly on things below.

Slowly, the shape of the Moon seems to change. We see less and less of it.

Days go by. The Moon looks thinner and thinner. Now only a bit of it can be seen.

Then, the Moon seems to disappear. It's still there, but we just can't see it.

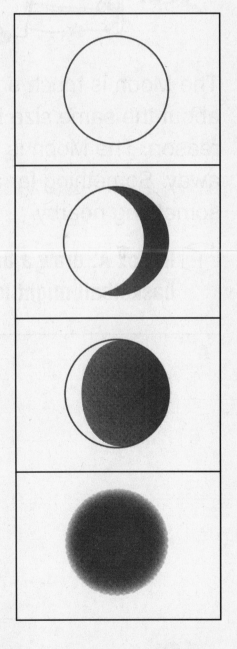

How Near? How Far?

The Moon is much smaller than the Sun. But they both look about the same size from the Earth. Why? Here is the reason. The Moon is near the Earth, and the Sun is far away. Something far away looks much smaller than something nearby.

In box A, draw a basketball. In box B, show how the basketball might look from far away.

A	B

We See the Moon

Find out how we can see the Moon at night. Do this activity.

1. Let someone hold a flashlight like this. Pretend the flashlight is the Sun.

2. Hold a white ball like this. Pretend the ball is the Moon. Pretend you are the Earth.

3. Earth, Moon, and Sun stand in a dark room like this.

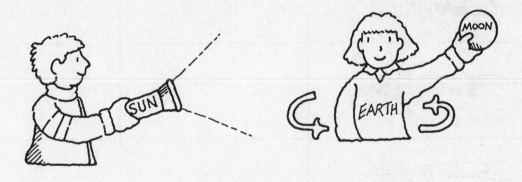

4. The Earth then turns slowly in a circle.

_____

_ _ _ _ _ _ _ _ _ _ _ _ _ _ _ _ _ _

5. Does the Moon make light? _____

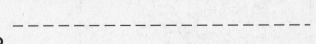

6. Why do we see the Moon?

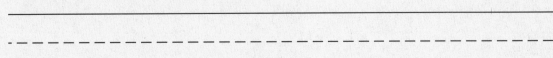

_____

_ _ _ _ _ _ _ _ _ _ _ _ _ _ _ _ _ _

_____

Comparing the Earth and the Moon

The Earth and the Moon are alike in some ways. They both have mountains. They both have rocks.

The Earth and Moon are also different in some ways. The Earth has air. The Moon has no air. The Earth has water. The Moon has no water.

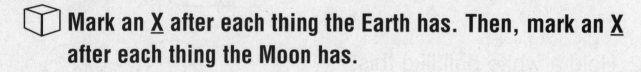 Mark an **X** after each thing the Earth has. Then, mark an **X** after each thing the Moon has.

	Earth	**Moon**

Moon Craters

The Moon is covered with many holes. These holes are called **craters**. The craters were made when rocks from space slammed into the Moon.

Some craters are so big that a whole city would fit into them. Other craters are small enough for an astronaut to jump across.

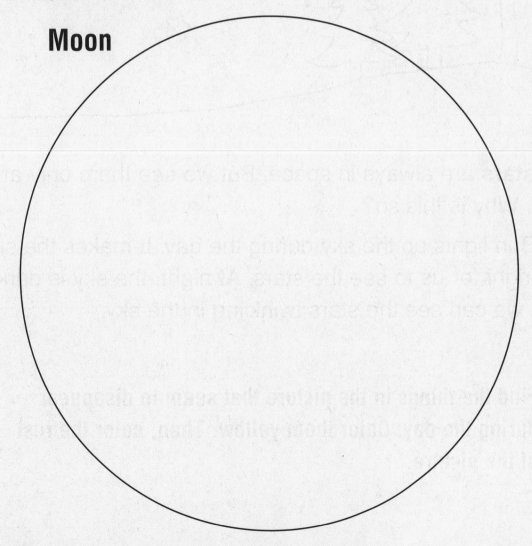

Complete the following.

1. Draw three big craters on the Moon below.
2. Then, draw six small craters on the Moon.
3. Color your picture.

Moon

Where Do the Stars Go?

The **stars** are always in space. But we see them only at night. Why is this so?

The Sun lights up the sky during the day. It makes the sky too bright for us to see the stars. At night, the sky is dark. Then we can see the stars twinkling in the sky.

Find the things in the picture that seem to disappear during the day. Color them yellow. Then, color the rest of the picture.

Billions of Stars

You can't count all the stars in the sky. There are too many! Some stars are bright. Others are dim. Some look very white or yellow. Others look kind of red or blue.

A star's color tells how hot it is. White and yellow stars are hotter than red stars. But blue stars are the hottest stars of all!

Sometimes people use a **telescope** to see stars better. It makes the stars look bigger.

▢ Complete the following.

1. Color the telescope in the picture black.

2. Color the stars red, yellow, white, and blue.

3. Mark an <u>X</u> on the hottest stars.

Pictures in the Sky

This is a **constellation**. A constellation is a group of stars that looks like a person, an animal, or an object.

The constellation in the picture is called the Big Dipper. A dipper is a cup with a long handle. People have made up stories about the Big Dipper. They have made up stories about other constellations in the sky, too.

◻ **Complete the following.**

1. Draw a blue line to show the cup of the Big Dipper.

2. Color the handle of the dipper black.

BACKGROUND INFORMATION

Living and Nonliving Things

All living things carry on activities that nonliving things do not. These life processes define a living thing. All living things grow, or increase in size and the amount of matter they contain. All living things can reproduce, or make more of the same kind of organism. Living things consume energy, change it, and excrete, or give off, waste. Living things react to stimuli and to changes in the environment.

Nonliving things may carry on some of these activities, but because they do not carry on all of these activities, they are not living. Students may be confused about what is living and what is not. Water seems to move, change, and appear alive. A flame will flicker and grow. Even scientists disagree about certain things, such as viruses. Distinguishing between living and nonliving things can be difficult, but students can follow the guidelines above to grasp the concept.

The Biosphere

The biosphere includes the atmosphere, the upper surface of the Earth's crust, and the oceans. The Sun can also be considered part of the biosphere, as its energy is used by living things. Life on Earth is contained in the biosphere. Here living things grow, reproduce, and die. In the process, they interact with each other, with other living and nonliving things, and with their environment. They change to adapt to their environments, and they change their environments. Any study of the biosphere includes the study of the relationships between the plants and animals that live there. The interactions between the plants and animals in the biosphere consist of energy chains, or food chains.

Life Cycles

All living things go through life cycles. From single-celled organisms to the largest animals, these life cycles include growth, change, consumption of food and water, use of energy, reproduction, and death. Reproduction varies among life forms. Plants reproduce by seeds or spores. Animals may lay eggs or give birth to live young. Some offspring resemble the parents and others do not. Some animals, such as frogs, undergo metamorphosis, or a complete change, during their lifetimes. The successful reproduction of a species is important to that population's continued growth or stability.

Plant Classification

The plant kingdom contains about 450,000 different kinds of plants, which are each classified into several divisions. The four main classifications for plants are: algae (almost all live in water; from microscopic single-celled plants to seaweed); bryophyta (mosses and liverworts; live in moist places; produce spores); pteridophyta (ferns, clubmosses, horsetails; no flowers); and permatophyta (largest group, with over 350,000 species; reproduce by way of seeds).

Flowering plants are the most numerous type of plant on Earth. They are further classified into groups. Some of the common groups of flowering plants are: grass family (corn, barley, rice, wheat);

lily family (violets, hyacinths, tulips, onions, asparagus); palm family (coconut, date); rose family (strawberries, peaches, cherries, apples, and other fruits); legume family (peas, beans, peanuts); beech family; and composite family (sunflowers and others with flowers that are actually many small flowers).

Plants are also classified as vascular and nonvascular. Vascular plants have tubes that bring the liquids the plants need from their environment up through the stalk. The tubes also help to support the plants. Nonvascular plants, such as mosses, do not have tubes. They are shorter because they must remain close to their source of moisture. They get the water and nutrients they need through their root systems.

Photosynthesis

Most plants are green. The reason that green plants are green is because they contain chlorophyll, most of which is in the leaves. There are some plants that contain chlorophyll but whose leaves are not green. This is because the chlorophyll has been masked by other pigmentation in the plant. Chlorophyll is necessary for the making of food, but the chlorophyll itself is not used in the food that is made.

Photosynthesis depends on light. A plant that is deprived of light loses its chlorophyll (and its ability to make food) and eventually will die. Plants take in the energy from the sun and carbon, carbon dioxide, and hydrogen from the air and water. They change these materials into carbohydrates and oxygen. The carbohydrates are used and stored in the plants for food. The oxygen is released into the air and water where the plants live. In this way, plants constantly replenish the Earth's oxygen supply.

Reproduction

Plants reproduce from seeds in flowers, from seeds in cones, or from spores. The seeds form after fertilization of their egg cells by male cells from pollen grains. Pollen can be carried to the egg cells by bees or other insects, by the wind, or by animals.

Seeds contain tiny plants called embryos around which a store of food is packed. In some seeds, such as bean seeds, the food is stored inside the embryo. Seeds are spread by animals and the wind. When the seeds in a cone are ripe, the cone will open, and the seeds will float to the ground or be carried by the wind. Some seeds have tiny parachutes to help them drift. A seed needs moisture, warmth, and oxygen to begin growing into a new plant. If conditions are not right for germination, some seeds can remain in a resting state for hundreds of years.

Pollination

The first thing people usually notice about a flower is its petals. The petals of a flower are brightly colored and designed to attract the insects that will help to pollinate it. When an insect comes to a flower to get nectar for itself, its body may touch the stamen of the flower. The stamen is covered with pollen that it has produced. The pollen is carried on the insect's body to the next flower. The pollen goes down the pollen tube in the pistil of the new flower. At the bottom of the pistil are the ovules, or the tiny beads that will grow into seeds. If the pollen is from the right type of flower, the ovules are fertilized and begin to grow. Some flowers can self-pollinate, but many prevent this from happening because their stigmas and stamens ripen at different times. Flowers that depend upon insects to carry their pollen are cross-pollinated.

Animal Classification

The animal kingdom can be classified into two large groups: the vertebrates (those with backbones) and the invertebrates (those without backbones). The backbone supports the body and provides flexibility. The spinal cord extends from the brain through the backbone, or spine. Individual nerves branch out from the spinal cord to different parts of the body. Messages from the brain are sent throughout the body through the spinal cord.

Some animals without backbones are sponges, jellyfish, clams, worms, insects, and spiders. Some of these animals have networks of nerves throughout their bodies with no central nerve cords. Many, like insects, have hard exoskeletons that protect their bodies and give them shape.

Animals are further categorized into six groups:

• Mammals are identified as animals that have hair or fur, feed milk to their young, and are warm-blooded. Warm-blooded animals are able to withstand a wide variety of temperatures and still keep their bodies warm, so they are found almost everywhere. Mammals are vertebrates and breathe through their lungs. Mammals' eggs are fertilized internally, and the babies are born alive. Mammals are capable of learning and have highly developed brains. Some mammals are carnivores (such as lions and dogs) and eat only animals, or meat; some are herbivores (such as rabbits and giraffes) and eat only plants; and some are omnivores (such as bears and skunks) and eat both animals and plants.

• Amphibians are animals that live both on land and in water. They are cold-blooded animals, most with smooth, wet skin. Most lay eggs in the water and move onto the land as they get older. Amphibians undergo a metamorphosis in which their form changes completely. For example, frogs lay their eggs in the water. The eggs grow into tadpoles with heads, gills, and no legs. Then, they develop two legs. Later they develop two more legs and lungs, and their tails begin to disappear. Finally, they have four fully grown legs, no tails, and no gills, and they leave the water to live on land. Most amphibians are herbivores when they are born and carnivores when they become adults living on land. Amphibians can breathe through their skin as well as with their lungs. Most amphibians with legs have webbed feet.

• Reptiles are scaly-skinned, cold-blooded animals. Their body temperatures vary with the temperature of the air around them. Reptiles get energy from the warmth of the Sun. They get sluggish when they are cold. Their skin feels dry and hard. Some reptiles have four legs, and some do not have any legs. Some reptiles bear live young, but most lay eggs. Baby reptiles look much like their parents and can care for themselves from birth. Although many reptiles can swim, they do not breathe under water. They breathe air with their lungs. Reptiles live in forests, jungles, and deserts.

• Birds are the only creatures with feathers. They are warm-blooded vertebrates. Most birds have hollow bones and powerful wing muscles that enable them to fly. Some, such as the ostrich, do not fly. Birds' eggs are fertilized in the body, a protective shell is formed, and the bird lays the eggs. Birds care for their young until they are able to fly and get their own food.

• Fish are fitted to their environment because of their gills, which enable them to absorb oxygen from the water. They use their fins and tails to move and are covered with scales. Fish reproduce by external fertilization; the female lays the eggs (spawns) and the male deposits sperm over the eggs. Fish are divided into three groups: jawless fish, cartilage fish, and bony fish. Fish are cold-blooded animals. Their bodies are the temperature of the water in which they live.

- Arthropods are animals without backbones. They have jointed legs, a segmented body, and an exoskeleton. Insects make up the majority of arthropods. Insects have three body parts: the head, the thorax, and the abdomen. The eyes, antennas, and mouths are on the head. Insects have six legs. Some have wings. All insects have a tough exoskeleton. This protects the insect's organs but must be shed as the insect grows. Insects undergo either a complete or incomplete metamorphosis as they develop from egg to maturity. A complete metamorphosis includes four stages: the egg, the larva, the pupa, and the adult. The incomplete metamorphosis includes an egg stage, a nymph stage, and the adult stage.

Metamorphosis

The life cycles of some animals include a metamorphosis. A metamorphosis is a complete change in the appearance of an animal. The most striking metamorphosis is the change from caterpillar to butterfly. Metamorphosis is controlled by hormones in the body. When the hormone supply keeping a caterpillar a juvenile stops, the caterpillar begins to become a chrysalis, or pupa. In a frog, the change is controlled by the thyroid gland. Crabs also undergo metamorphosis, and earwigs and grasshoppers undergo incomplete metamorphosis.

Health

Health for children revolves around healthy foods, plenty of exercise, and good hygiene. As children grow, they should begin to recognize that they can make choices that will help them live healthy lives. They need to learn the connections between what they eat and the way they look and feel. They need to have the basic information that will help them to make

good food choices. Children need to know that it is never too early to begin healthy habits in eating, exercise, and hygiene. The habits they form now will affect their lives for many years to come.

Nutrition

The body needs to receive certain nutrients in order to grow and to stay healthy. These nutrients are broken down into six types: carbohydrates, protein, fat, vitamins, minerals, and water.

- Carbohydrates are sugars and starches. Sugars, such as fruits and honey, give the body quick energy while the starches, such as bread, cereal, and rice, give the body stored energy.

- Proteins come from foods such as milk, cheese, lean meat, fish, peas, and beans. They help the body to repair itself. Proteins are used by the body to build muscle and bone, and they give the body energy.

- Fat is important for energy, too, and it helps to keep the body warm, but if the body does not use the fats put into it, it will store the fat. Fats come from foods such as meat, milk, butter, oil, and nuts.

- Vitamins are important to the body in many ways. Vitamins help the other nutrients in a person's body work together. Lack of certain vitamins can cause serious illnesses. Vitamin A, for example, from foods such as broccoli, carrots, radishes, and liver, helps with eyesight. Vitamin B from green leafy vegetables, eggs, and milk, helps with growth and energy. Vitamin C from citrus fruits, cauliflower, strawberries, tomatoes, peppers, and broccoli, prevents sickness.

- Milk, vegetables, liver, seafood, and raisins are some of the foods that provide the minerals necessary for growth. Calcium is a mineral that helps with strong bones, and iron is needed for healthy red blood.

- Water makes up most of the human body and helps to keep our temperature normal. It is healthy and recommended to drink several glasses of water each day.

Foods have long been divided into four basic food groups: meat, milk, vegetable-fruit, and bread-cereal. New discoveries have led to a change in the divisions so that in a food pyramid, fruits and vegetables are separated, and fats are included at the top of the pyramid. The recommended servings for each group have also changed over time. Eating the right amount of foods from each group each day gives one a balanced diet. Eating too many foods from one group or not enough of another can lead to deficiencies or weight problems. Although vitamin supplements can help with these deficiencies, vitamins are best absorbed in the body naturally through the digestion of the foods that contain them.

- The Bread-Cereal (Grain) Group contains foods made from grains such as wheat, corn, rice, oats, and barley. Six to eleven servings from this group each day give you carbohydrates, vitamins, and minerals.

- The Vegetable and Fruit Groups contain vitamins, minerals, and carbohydrates. Two to four servings of fruits and three to five servings of vegetables each day are recommended.

- The Meat Group includes chicken, fish, red meats, peas, nuts, and eggs. The meat group contains much of the protein we get from our diets, but it also includes fats. Two to three servings from the meat group each day are recommended.

- The Milk Group includes milk (whole and skim), butter, cheese, yogurt, and ice cream and gives us fat, vitamins, protein, and minerals that are important for strong bones and teeth. Two to three servings from the milk group each day are recommended.

- The Fats, Oils, and Sweets Group, including butter, oil, and margarine, should be used sparingly.

Hygiene

Keeping the body clean is an important part of staying healthy. Children need to know that when they wash, they are washing off viruses and bacteria, or germs, which can cause illness. Washing the hair and body regularly prevents bacteria from entering the skin through cuts and from getting into the mouth. Hands should always be washed after handling garbage or using the bathroom. Regular brushing and flossing can help keep teeth healthy.

Germs can also come from other people. Children should be discouraged from sharing straws, cups, or other utensils. They should be reminded to always cover their mouths when they sneeze or cough, and to use tissues frequently. Children also need to be reminded not to share combs or hats.

Exercise and Sleep

Muscles grow when they are used and contract when they are not used. Muscles that become unaccustomed to exercise can be injured by sudden or strenuous activity. This is why muscles should be exercised regularly and in moderation. Occasional strenuous activity is not advantageous to the muscles and does not give long-term results. Exercising the muscles makes the body grow larger and stronger and helps make the heart strong.

Regular exercise can relax the body and help people get a good night's rest. Sleep is an important part of keeping the body healthy. People need different amounts of sleep at different times of their lives. Babies sleep most of the time because their bodies are growing very quickly. School children usually require from eight to ten hours of sleep, and adults need about seven or eight hours. Sleep allows the body and mind to rest. If we don't get enough sleep, our bodies and minds do not function as well as they should. Our attention wanders, and we become forgetful. Our muscles will feel weak and less coordinated. Lack of sleep can also make people irritable and impair their judgment.

The Five Senses and the Nervous System

The human body collects information using the five senses: sight, smell, hearing, taste, and touch. The nervous system enables us to put all of our senses together so that messages are sent to the brain and we are able to act according to the information that the brain receives. The nervous system enables us to react. It controls all of the other systems in the body.

The major organ of the nervous system is the brain. Another part of the nervous system is a system of nerves that carry information to the brain. The third part of the nervous system is the sense organs. For example, the nose is the sense organ for the sense of smell. There are many nerve cells in the nose that take the information regarding odors to a main nerve called the olfactory nerve. The olfactory nerve carries the information to your brain. Your brain will then tell your body what to do with the information.

RELATED READING

- *About Reptiles: A Guide for Children* by Cathryn P. Sill (Peachtree, 1999).

- *Animals on the Go* by Jessica Brett (Green Light Books, 2000).

- *Bananas!* by Jacqueline Farmer (Charlesbridge, 1999).

- *Bats, Bats, Bats* by Christine Price (Steck-Vaughn, 1997).

- *Bear Facts* by Gare Thompson (Steck-Vaughn, 1997).

- *Bugs Are Insects* by Anne Rockwell (*Let's-Read-and-Find-Out Science Series,* HarperCollins, 2001).

- *Crawdad Creek* by Scott Russell Sanders (National Geographic, 1999).

- *Festival Foods Around the World* by Becky Stull (Steck-Vaughn, 1997).

- *Growing Up Wild: Penguins* by Sandra Markle (Atheneum, 2001).

- *How Do They Grow? Series* by Jillian Powell (Raintree Steck-Vaughn, 2002).

Unit 3 Assessment

 **Circle the things that living things need.**

1.

 **Tell how each animal moves. Write <u>hop</u>, <u>swim</u>, <u>walk</u>, or <u>fly</u> under each picture.**

2.

_____   _____   _____   _____

 Look at each picture. Write which sense you would use the most. Write <u>see</u>, <u>hear</u>, <u>smell</u>, <u>touch</u>, or <u>taste</u>.

3.

_____   _____   _____   _____

GO ON TO THE NEXT PAGE 👉

Unit 3 Assessment, p. 2

◻ **Label the parts of the plant with the words.**

| stem | roots | leaf | flower |

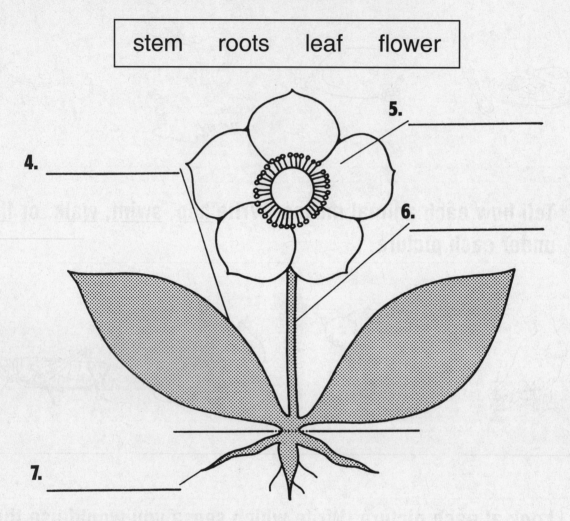

5. _____

4. _____

6. _____

7. _____

◻ **Complete the following.**

8. Write **a** on the part of the plant that makes food.

9. Write **b** on the part of the plant that carries food and water through the plant.

10. Write **c** on the part of the plant that carries water from the soil to the plant.

11. Write **d** on the part of the plant that makes seeds.

Living or Not Living?

All things are made of matter. Matter can be **living** or not living.

◻ **Cut out the pictures at the bottom of the page.**
Paste them on the chart where they belong.

Living	Not Living

Living Things Grow

Living things grow. They need food, water, and air to grow.

 **Cut out the pictures. On another sheet of paper, paste them in order. Show how a plant grows. Show how an animal grows.**

Find the Living Things

Living things are all around.

[cube icon] **Find the living things. Put a green circle around plants. Put a red circle around animals. Put an X on things that are not living.**

Are Seeds Living Things?

Seeds grow into plants. Are seeds living things? Let's find out.

You will need
- ☆ water   ☆ spoon   ☆ clear plastic cup
- ☆ seeds   ☆ potting soil

1. Put some soil in a cup.

2. Put some seeds in the soil.

3. Water the seeds.

4. Start your chart.

5. Wait a few days.

6. Complete your chart.

| Kind of seed: _____ |
| Date planted: _____ |
| Date I saw leaves: _____ |
| Date I saw stem: _____ |

🔲 **Answer the questions.**

1. Are the seeds growing?

_____

_____

_____

2. Are seeds living things?

_____

_____

_____

_____

What Grows on a Farm?

Many living things grow on a farm.

Circle the plants in green.
Circle the animals in red.
Then, color the rest of the picture.

Plant Parts

Can you name each plant part?

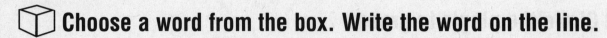 **Choose a word from the box. Write the word on the line.**

flower   stem   leaf   roots

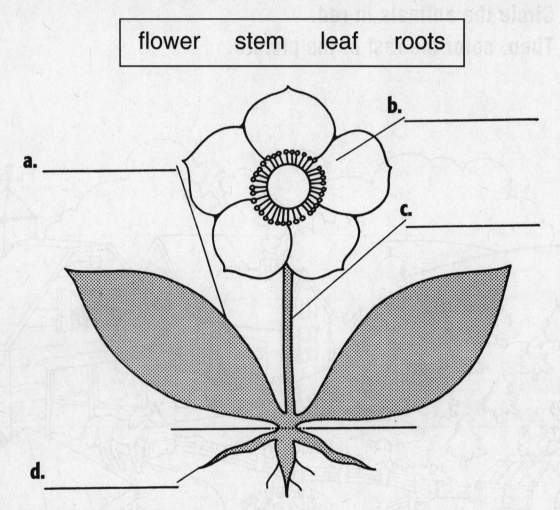

a. _____

b. _____

c. _____

d. _____

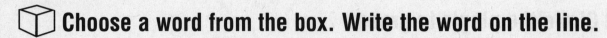 **Complete each sentence.**

1. Water goes up the root to the _____.

2. _____ hold the plant in the ground.

Look at a Plant

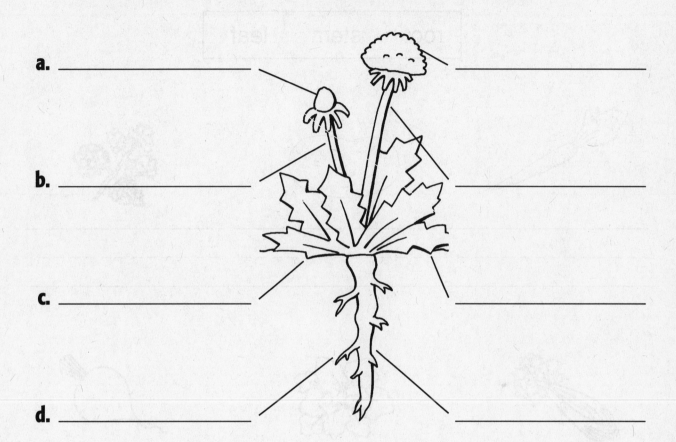 **Cut out the words and sentences below.**
Paste each one where it belongs. Color the plant.

a. _____   _____

b. _____   _____

c. _____   _____

d. _____   _____

stem	leaf	root	flower
This part makes food for the plant.		This part carries food and water through the plant.	
This part makes seeds.		This part carries water from the soil to the plant.	

Parts of Plants

Look at each picture. Does it show a root, stem, or leaf?

 Write one of these words under each picture.

root	stem	leaf

_____

- - - - - - - - - - - - - -

_____

_____

- - - - - - - - - - - - - -

_____

_____

- - - - - - - - - - - - - -

_____

Plant Puzzle

 **Write the word for each picture in the puzzle.**

Down

1.

2.

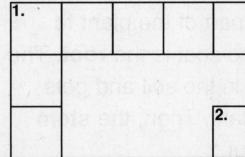

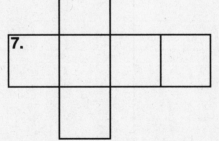

6.

Across

1.   **3.**   **4.**   **5.**   **7.**

Seeds Sprout

When the **embryo** of a seed begins to come out of its seed coat, we say that it "sprouts." Seeds need water and warmth to **sprout**. The first part of the plant to come out of the seed coat is the **root**. The root holds the plant in the soil and gets water for the new plant. Then, the **stem** and **leaves** come out.

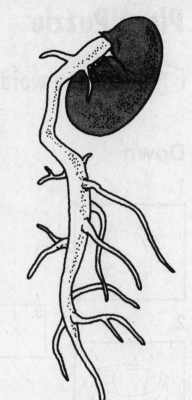

In the first box, draw a seed in the soil. In the second box, draw what the seed looks like when it sprouts.

1.	2.

How Do Seeds Grow?

Do you know how seeds grow? Let's find out.

┌─ **You will need** ─────────────────────────────┐
☆ clear plastic cups	☆ paper towels
☆ lima bean or corn seeds	☆ spray bottle
☆ drawing paper	☆ crayons
└──┘

1. Put a paper towel in a cup.
2. Put a little water in the cup.
3. Place bean seeds between the paper and the cup.
4. Keep the towel damp. Watch the seeds change.
5. Draw a picture of them every day.

📦 **Answer the questions.**

1. Which part grows first?

_____

_ _ _ _ _ _ _ _ _ _ _ _ _ _ _ _ _

_____

2. What plant parts grow from seeds?

_____

_ _ _ _ _ _ _ _ _ _ _ _ _ _ _ _ _

_____

_____

_ _ _ _ _ _ _ _ _ _ _ _ _ _ _ _ _

_____

What Do Plants Need?

Do seeds need soil to sprout? Do plants need soil to grow? Let's find out.

You will need

☆ 6 lima bean seeds   ☆ 2 jars
☆ small stones   ☆ soil
☆ water

1. Put 3 lima bean seeds in a jar of stones.

2. Put enough water in the jar of stones to cover the lower half of the seeds.

3. Put 3 seeds in a jar of soil.

4. Water the seeds.

5. Put both jars in sunlight.

6. Watch the seeds for 2 weeks.

📦 **Answer the questions.**

1. Do seeds need soil to sprout?

_____

– –

_____

2. Do plants need soil to grow?

_____

– –

_____

How Plants Grow

Do you know how plants grow? Show what you know.

📦 **Cut out the pictures at the bottom of the page.**
   Paste them in order here.

📦 **Complete the sentences to tell how to grow a plant. Use words from the box.**

plants   seeds   flowers

_____

_ _ _ _ _ _ _ _ _ _ _ _ _ _ _

1. We plant _____ in a pot.

_____

_ _ _ _ _ _ _ _ _ _ _ _ _ _ _

2. Soon, small _____ begin to grow.

_____

_ _ _ _ _ _ _ _ _ _ _ _ _ _ _

3. The plants may grow pretty _____.

How a Greenhouse Works

A **greenhouse** is a warm place for plants to grow. Do you know how a greenhouse works?

Cut out the labels at the bottom of the page. Paste them in place in the picture.

Plants need sunlight. Glass lets the sunlight in.	Plants need water. They are being watered.
Plants need to be warm. The heater keeps them warm.	Plants need air. Open windows let air in.

Kinds of Animals

Animals are all around us. Do you know how animals are alike?

 Look at each row of pictures. Put an X on the animal that does not belong.

1.

2.

3.

4.

 Answer the question.

_____

5. Which is the largest animal? _____

What Do Animals Eat?

Animals must eat **food** to stay alive.
What kinds of foods do animals eat?

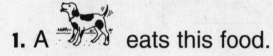 **Complete each sentence.**
   Look at books or ask an adult to help you.

1. A 🐕 eats this food.

_____

It is made from _____.

2. A 🐈 eats _____.

3. A 🐟 eats _____.

4. A 🦅 eats _____.

5. A 🐁 eats _____.

How Do Birds Find Food?

Birds are animals. They must eat food to live. How do birds find food? Let's find out.

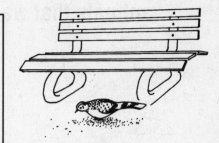

> **You will need**
> - ⭐ string
> - ⭐ nail
> - ⭐ plastic cup
> - ⭐ $\frac{1}{2}$ cup of bird seed
> - ⭐ $\frac{1}{4}$ cup of peanut butter

1. Punch holes near the rim of the plastic cup. Tie the string to the top of the cup so that it can be hung outside.

2. Mix the peanut butter and bird seed together.

3. Put it in the cup.

4. Hang the cup outside. You have made a bird feeder! (Note: Do not feed birds peanut butter alone. It can clog their air passages.)

📦 Answer the questions.

1. How did the birds eat the food?

_____

_____

_____

2. How do birds find food?

_____

_____

_____

Fly, Walk, or Swim?

Animals move in different ways.

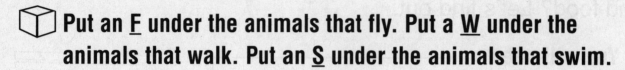 **Put an F under the animals that fly. Put a W under the animals that walk. Put an S under the animals that swim.**

1. _____   2. _____   3. _____

4. _____   5. _____   6. _____

7. _____   8. _____   9. _____

Hairy Animals

What do you know about **mammals**? Some are big. Some are small. Some walk or run. Others swing in trees. But mammals are alike in one way. A mammal has **hair** on its body. The hair can be thick or thin. The rabbit's hair is thick. It is called **fur**. Fur helps keep the rabbit warm. A sheep has thick hair called **wool**. The elephant, the whale, and the monkey have thin hair.

Color the animals that are mammals.

1.

2.

3.

4.

5.

6.

Reptiles

These animals are different in many ways. Some walk on four legs. Others crawl because they have no legs at all. Some spend most of their time in water. Others spend their time on land. But these animals are alike in one important way. They are all **reptiles**.

Reptiles are animals that have a body covered with **scales**. Snakes and lizards have scales that cover their whole body. Turtles have hard scales that make a shell.

Answer the question.

What is a reptile's body covered with?

_____

_ _

_____

Reptiles Are Cool (and Warm)

A mammal's body usually stays warm, even when it is in cold air. But a reptile's body does not. A reptile will become as warm or as cool as the air around it. On a cool day, a reptile will lie in the sunlight to get warm. On a hot day, the reptile will look for shade.

It is a very cool day. Draw an X where a reptile will most likely be.

It is a very hot day. Draw an X where a reptile will most likely be.

Fish

fins

mouth

gills

tail

Fish have body parts that help them move about in the water. This fish swings its **tail** from side to side. That helps it move forward. A fish uses its **fins** to turn left or right.

Fish open and close their mouths. They also open and close their **gills**. This helps water flow through their gills. Fish use their gills to get air from the water.

Label the parts of the fish. Use the words <u>gills</u>, <u>fin</u>, and <u>tail</u>. Write a word in each box.

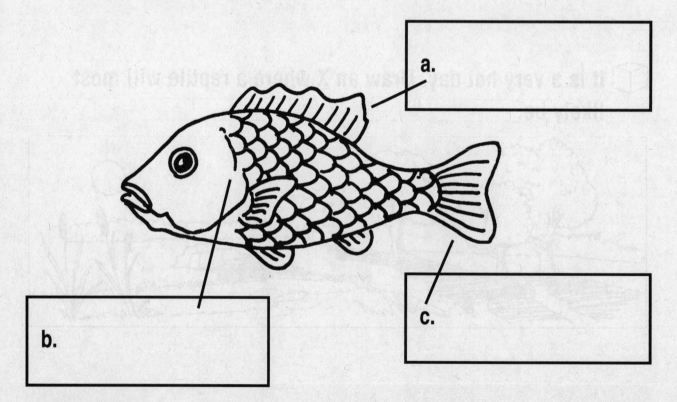

a.

b.

c.

Fishy Facts

Fish are animals that have gills. Most fish also have fins. Fish live in water. Some live in **fresh water**. Other fish live in **salt water**.

◻ **Circle all the words that tell about fish.**

feathers	tail	whale
gills	milk	shark
water	swim	wings
fins	fly	swim bladder

◻ **Draw a picture of a fish.**

Birds

All **birds** have **wings**. They use their wings to help them fly. The bird uses its legs to push off the ground or a tree. At the same time, it begins to flap its wings. Sometimes a bird can stop flapping once it is high in the air. It can glide in the wind. Then, it flaps when it wants to turn or stop.

All birds have wings, but not all birds can fly. The penguin can swim underwater, but it cannot fly. The ostrich can run faster than a person, but it cannot fly.

Color the parts of these birds that help them fly.

Fine Feathers

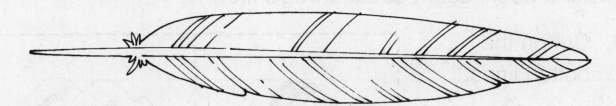

All birds have **feathers**. Feathers can be tiny or large. Some feathers have only one color. Others are made of many colors.

When you look at a feather, you may notice that one side is shiny. This is because oil from the bird's body is on the feather. The oil makes the feather look shiny.

▢ Finish this picture of a feather.

It's a Frog's Life

Make a book. Learn about a frog's life.

1. Cut on the dotted lines.

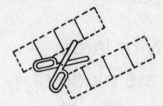

2. Fold in half. Tape the ends together.

3. Fold in half again. Put the two parts together.

4. Staple.

A frog lays eggs in the water. Tadpoles hatch from the eggs.

Tadpoles live in the water. They begin to grow legs.

Mini-Book
How a Frog Grows

This book belongs to _____

A tadpole grows to look like a frog.

Insects

Insects have six legs, three body parts, and two feelers. Some of these animals below are insects. Some are not.

🔳 **Circle the animals that are insects. Mark an X on the animals that are not insects.**

1.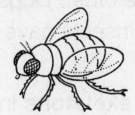

2.

3.

4.

5.

6.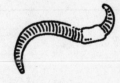

7.

8.

9.

10.

Don't Bug Me!

Snakes and fish have no legs. Birds have two legs. Dogs and cats have four legs. Insects have six legs!

Snakes and fish have one main body part. Birds have two. The head is one part, and the body is the other. Dogs and cats have two main body parts, too. But insects have three main body parts.

Snakes, fish, birds, dogs, and cats have **skeletons** inside their bodies. But insects do not! They wear their skeletons on the outside of their bodies.

Draw your own insect. Be sure it has all the parts insects must have.

Animals in Danger

There are few of these animals left.

whale

seal

elephant

eagle

 Write their names in the puzzle below.

Across

1. This is a large animal with large ears.

2. This animal uses its flippers to swim.

Down

3. This is the largest animal that lives in water.

4. This large bird has sharp claws.

They're Everywhere!

Animals are everywhere. They live in **forests**. They live in **oceans** and **ponds**. Animals live in **deserts**, too.

Find all the animals in this picture of a forest.
Color each mammal yellow.
Circle the birds.
Color the fish green.
Color the reptiles brown.
Draw a square around the insect.

Animal Aptitude

How many animals do you know?

◻ **What kind of animal is it? Write a word from the box next to each picture.**

mammal	bird	fish	reptile	insect

1. _____

_____

2. _____

_____

3. _____

_____

4. _____

_____

5. _____

_____

GO ON TO THE NEXT PAGE 👉

Animal Aptitude, p. 2

 **What kind of animal is it? Write a word from the box next to each picture.**

mammal	bird	fish	reptile	insect

6.  _____

7. _____

8. _____

9. _____

10. _____

People Grow and Change

People get older. They grow and **change**.

 **Circle what people need to grow.**

 **Draw your hair now. Then, draw how it will look if it is not cut.**

 **Circle the adult.**

Color the one that is close to your age.

Do We All Grow the Same?

Everybody grows. Do we all grow the same? Let's find out.

┌─── **You will need** ──────────────────┐
   ☆ meter stick   ☆ paper   ☆ pencil
└──┘

1. Measure the height of all the students in the class.

2. Write each height on a piece of paper.

📦 **Answer the questions.**

1. How tall is the tallest student?

_____

- -

_____

2. How tall is the shortest student?

_____

- -

_____

3. How many different heights are the students in your classroom?

_____

- -

_____

4. Does every person grow the same?

_____

- -

_____

How Have You Changed?

You have changed, too. Let's find out how you have changed.

You will need
☆ baby picture   ☆ paper   ☆ crayons   ☆ mirror
---

1. Bring your baby picture to school.

2. Draw a picture of yourself now. Use a mirror.

📦 **Answer the questions.**

1. How has your weight changed?

_____

- -

_____

2. How else have you changed?

_____

- -

_____

3. How do you think you will look next year?

_____

- -

_____

_____

- -

_____

How Do You Measure Growth?

People grow taller. They **weigh** more.
You can measure **growth**.

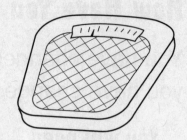

┌─ **You will need** ──────────────────┐
│ ☆ bathroom scale   ☆ meter stick │
└──────────────────────────────────────┘

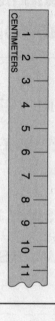

1. Use a scale to measure your weight.

2. Use a meter stick to measure your height.

📦 **Answer the questions.**

1. How much do you weigh?

_____

- -

_____

2. How tall are you?

_____

- -

_____

3. How else can you measure growth?

_____

- -

_____

- -

_____

Your Senses

Most people have five **senses**. They can see, hear, feel, smell, and taste.

⬜ **Look at the first picture in each row. Circle all the senses you can use.**

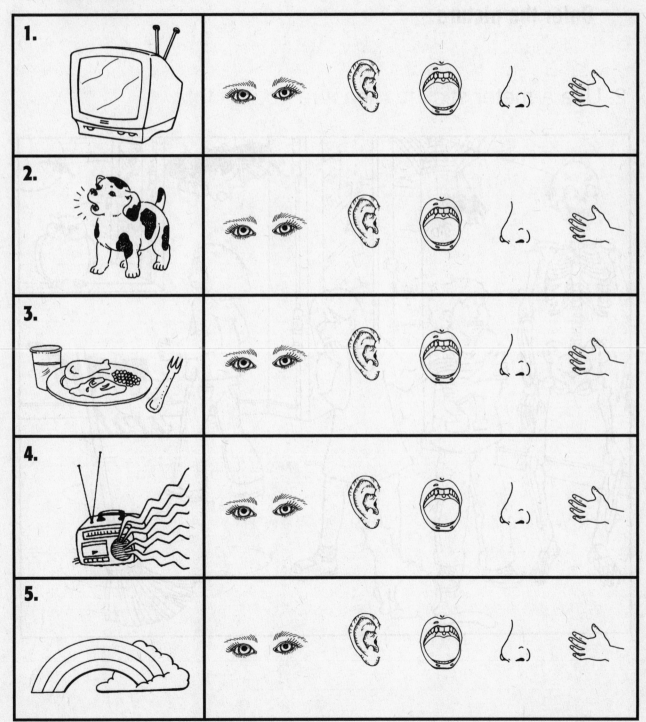

Spooky Senses

Talk about the picture.
What do you see?
What do you hear?
What do you feel?
Color the picture.

Using Your Senses

We use our senses to **observe** things. What do you observe?

⬛ **Complete the sentences.**

Today is _____.

I was in a store on _____.

I saw _____.

I heard _____.

I smelled _____.

I felt _____.

I tasted _____.

Food Sense

Do you like food? Which senses do you use when you eat?

┌─ **You will need** ──────────────────────────────────────┐
│   ☆ unusual foods   ☆ knife   ☆ napkins   ☆ paper plates │
└──┘

1. Look at the food.

2. Touch, smell, taste, and listen to the food. (How does it sound when you eat it?)

 **Answer the questions.**

1. What did you find out about the food?

_____

- -

_____

- -

_____

2. Which senses did you use?

_____

- -

_____

- -

_____

People Need Food

People eat many kinds of food. Some foods come from animals. Some foods come from plants.

⬜ **Write A on foods from animals. Write P on foods from plants.**

Foods for Health

Some foods are good for you. Some foods are not so good.

🔲 **Color the foods that are best for you. Circle their names.**

milk

fish

candy

apple

soda

vegetables

cake

nuts

cereal

What We Need

The pictures show what we need.

🧊 **Draw a line from the pictures to the right words.**

1.

food

2.

water

3.

air

4.

rest

5.

play

Take Care of Your Eyes

Look at the pictures. Some pictures show good eye care.
Some pictures show poor eye care.

Put an **X** over the pictures that show poor eye care.

A

B

C

D

E

F

My Health-Care Record

How **healthy** are you? Keep a chart for a week. An adult can help you do this.

◻ **Keep this record for one week.**

	Wash my face.	Wash my hands.	Brush my teeth.	Comb my hair.	Eat breakfast.
Sunday					
Monday					
Tuesday					
Wednesday					
Thursday					
Friday					
Saturday					

Eating Well

To be healthy, you need many different foods. The boxes below name different food groups. Do you eat the right number of servings from each group?

📦 **Draw three foods for each group. Then, color your drawings.**

Vegetables and Fruits	**Bread and Cereal**
Eat four servings each day.	Eat four servings each day.
Meat and Beans	**Milk**
Eat two servings each day.	Eat two servings each day.

Staying Healthy

You can do things to stay healthy.

📦 **Some of the people are staying healthy.**
Draw a circle around them.
Some of the people are not staying healthy.
Draw an X over them.

A

B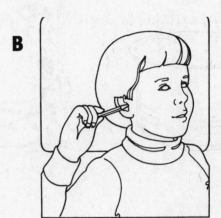

C

D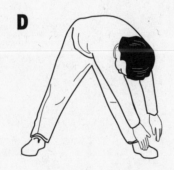

E

F

G

Staying Safe

Your eyes and ears help you stay **safe**.

🔲 **Look at the pictures. What helps you stay safe? Write <u>eyes</u>, <u>ears</u>, or <u>both</u> under each picture.**

1. _____

2. _____

3. _____

4. _____

5. _____

6. _____

Science Grade 1 Answer Key

Pages 4–6
1. false, 2. true, 3. true, 4. false,
5. false, 6. true, 7. no, 8. yes,
9. soil, 10. air, 11. wind, 12. Sun,
13. dark, 14. Students should
circle the fish and the cat.,
15. grass, P; tree, P; bird, A; dog,
A, 16. Students should circle the
mouse, draw a line under the
fish, draw an X on the bird, draw
a triangle around the snake, and
draw a square around the bug.,
17. Students should circle fruit,
corn, and milk.

Pages 13–14
1. liquid, 2. solid, 3. gas,
4. gravity, 5. force, 6. Students
should circle the nail and the
pin., 7. Check that students have
colored the ends of the magnets.,
8. push, 9. push, 10. pull

Page 15
Answers may vary.
1. shiny, 2. smooth, 3. hard,
4. dull, 5. soft, 6. rough

Page 16
Answers will vary.

Page 18
1. Answers will vary.,
2. Answers will vary.

Page 20
1. Answers will vary.,
2. Answers will vary.

Page 21
Red: lamp, picture, shelf, items
on shelf, dresser, chair, bed, fish
in tank, legs on tank; Blue: water
in glass, water in tank

Page 22
Students circle crayon, ring,
whistle, mitt.

Page 23
Students circle tub with water,
paints, fountain, water hose,
pool.

Page 24
Students circle cloud with wind,
soap bubbles, balloon, hair dryer
air, steam.

Page 25
1. solid, 2. liquid, 3. gas,
4. matter

Page 26
1. They melted., 2. The sunlight
or warm air

Page 28
1. There is less water in the pan
each day., 2. heat, warmth,
3. The water goes into the air as
a gas.

Page 30
1. Yes: The balloon near the heat
got bigger. The balloon in the
cold got smaller., 2. Cold makes
air get smaller., 3. Heat makes air
get larger.

Page 31
1. pull, 2. push, 3. push, 4. pull,
5. pull, 6. push

Page 32
Students color the lawn mower
and airplane. Students circle the
horse pull toy.

Page 34
Answers may vary.; 1. 1 hand,
2. 2 hands, 3. It was harder to
push 10 books because they were
heavier.

Page 36
1. smooth, 2. rough, 3. It was
harder to pull the block over the
pebbles because the pebbles were
rough. They rubbed more on the
bottom of the block. They made
more friction.

Page 37
1. a hard push, 2. a gentle push

Page 38
Students color the tricycle, lawn
mower, baby stroller, skateboard,
airplane, duck, bus.

Page 39
Students color the sailboat and
kite.

Page 40
Students should color the canoe,
raft, leaves, muddy feet, and
waterwheel toy.

Page 41
1. wind, 2. wind and water,
3. water, 4. wind and water,
5. wind

Page 42
Students write an X on the ground
under each block.

Page 43
1. 40 pounds, 2. Students color Ei.

Page 44
1. force, 2. heavy, 3. light,
4. gravity

Page 45
1. brick, 2. book, 3. bowl of
apples, 4. barbells

Page 46
Across: 1. push, 5. water,
6. gravity;
Down: 2. heavy, 3. air,
4. force

Page 48
Things a magnet pulls: nail,
paper clip, washer; Things a
magnet does not pull: comb,
rubber band, pencil, penny; 1. It
pulls things with iron., 2. It does
not pull things made from other
materials., 3. They all have iron.

Page 50
1. S and N, N and S; 2. S and S,
N and N; 3. Like poles push
apart.

Page 52
1. The poles hold the most clips.,
2. The poles are the strongest.

Page 54
1. Yes, 2. Answers will vary.,
3. The nail will pick up clips, but
it is not as strong as a magnet.

Page 56
1. Answers will vary.,
2. Answers will vary.,
3. Possible answers: The magnet
will not be as strong. It will lose
some of its force.

Page 57
1. cranes, 2. electromagnet,
3. force

Page 58

Across: **5.** magnet, **6.** repel;
Down: **1.** iron, **2.** cranes,
3. attract, **4.** poles

Page 60

1. Students should say "yes.",
2. The magnetic force transferred
to the needle makes it point north.

Page 61

1. holds things together, **2.** moves
things around, **3.** picks up things

Pages 69–70

1. true, **2.** true, **3.** false, **4.** true,
5. false, **6.** true, **7.** false, **8.** true,
9. sand, **10.** water,
11. temperature, **12.** turns,
13. day

Page 71

Students should color large rocks
yellow, small rocks blue, smooth
rocks red, and rough rocks green.
Rocks can be more than one
color.

Page 72

Things made of rocks: buildings,
road with stones on it, stone
bridge over stream, stone wall
lining stream, statue, cement
sidewalk, stones on ground and
in stream

Page 74

1. Bits of the soft rocks broke
off., **2.–3.** Answers will vary.

Page 75

4. Yes, the rocks got smaller.

Page 76

Drawings will vary.

Page 77

Rock parts:
1. pebbles, **2.** sand, **3.** dust;
Animal parts:
1. bones, **2.** feathers, **3.** shells,
4. insects, **5.** worms;
Plant parts:
1. leaves, **2.** roots, **3.** wood,
4. petals

Page 78

Drawings should show holes
underground for air and water,
rock parts, animal parts, and
plant parts.

Page 79

1. sand, **2.** clay, **3.** potting soil

Page 80

Yes, plants would grow well in
potting soil because it is a
mixture of clay and sand.

Page 81

Sand is different colors because
it comes from different colored
rocks.

Page 82

Answers will vary.

Page 83

1. on Earth, **2.** long, long ago,
3. no, **4.** They died out.

Page 84

1. b, **2.** c, **3.** a

Page 85

1. c, **2.** b, **3.** a

Page 86

1. wind, **2.** wind, water,
3. wind

Page 87

1. Color the boat on the left.,
2. larger sails

Page 88

Circle these things: kite, hot-air
balloon, sailboat, balloons,
bicycle, basketball, bubbles.

Page 89

1. feel, **2.** wind, **3.** cool, **4.** clean,
5. breathe

Page 90

Left picture: It is a wet day. The
wind is blowing. The air feels
cool.; Right picture: It is a dry
day. It is not windy. The air feels
warm.

Page 91

Pictures must show in order that
the Sun makes water go into the
air, then the evaporating water
builds up in clouds, then the
clouds produce rain.

Page 92

All four pictures in the top row
belong with the sunny picture on
the left. All four pictures in the
bottom row belong with the rainy
picture on the right. Left picture:
cotton balls; good weather or
sunny weather. Right picture:
dark, rain clouds; rainy weather.

Page 93

1. clouds, **2.** water, **3.** dark,
4. white, **5.** change

Page 94

1. cold, **2.** warm

Page 95

Temperatures will vary.

Page 96

Draw lines to match coat and
gloves to snowy scene, raincoat
and umbrella to rainy scene,
shorts and shirt to sunny scene,
sweatsuit to the windy scene.

Page 98

1.–2. Answers will vary.,
3. Students may say they used
today's weather to help predict
tomorrow's weather, or they may
say they listened to a forecast on
radio or TV.

Page 99

Students should underline 1, 2,
and 4.

Page 100

Drawings should show a line
around the Sun., **1.** orbit, **2.** year

Page 101

1. day, **2.** day and night

Page 102

At top of page: The Sun should
be drawn to the right. At bottom
of page: Color the right half of
the Earth.

Page 103

Students should circle the lamp,
flashlight, candle, stove, fire,
fireplace, space heater or
radiator.

Page 104

Students should color the top
picture with the Sun.

Page 105

1. light, **2.** Earth, **3.** day, **4.** turns

Page 106

big = peanut;
bigger = orange;
biggest = watermelon

Page 107

1. The shadow is on the ground to the left of the stick., **2.** The shadow is shorter and has moved more toward the center., **3.** The shadow has moved to the right of the stick., **4.** The shadow is longer and has moved more to the right.

Page 108

Students should circle line 2 and line 3.

Page 109

Students should color the Moon yellow and the sky black.

Page 110

A. Drawing shows a basketball., B. Drawing shows a smaller basketball than in A.

Page 111

5. no, **6.** Light from the Sun shines on the Moon. We see the light that shines on the Moon.

Page 112

Earth has rocks, mountains, water, and air. The Moon has rocks, mountains, no water, and no air.

Page 113

Drawings should show 3 large craters and 6 small craters.

Page 114

Students should color the stars yellow.

Page 115

1. Students should color the telescope black., **2.** Students should color the stars red, yellow, white, and blue., **3.** Students should mark an X on the blue (hottest) stars.

Page 116

1. Students should outline the cup of the Big Dipper in blue., **2.** Students should color the handle of the Big Dipper black.

Pages 123–124

1. Students should circle the food, water, and air., **2.** eagle, fly; cat, walk; shark, swim; grasshopper, hop; **3.** Senses: Answers may vary.; kitten, touch; radio, hear; ice cream, taste; rainbow, see; rose, smell.; Plant parts: **4.** leaf, **5.** flower, **6.** stem, **7.** roots; **8.** Student should write **a** on the leaf., **9.** Students should write **b** on the stem., **10.** Students should write **c** on the roots. **11.** Students should write **d** on the flower.

Page 125

Living: girl, plant, rabbit, bee; Not Living: rock, glass, chair, bread

Page 126

Check students' work for correct order.

Page 127

Green circle: 4 trees, bush, grass; Red circle: people, 2 elephants, 2 giraffes, 3 monkeys; X: benches, buildings, walls, fence, monkey tower, sidewalk, sky

Page 128

1. yes, **2.** Seeds are living things at rest. When given water, light, and soil, they grow.

Page 129

Check students' work.

Page 130

a. leaf, **b.** flower, **c.** stem, **d.** root, **1.** stem, **2.** Roots

Page 131

a. flower; This part makes seeds., **b.** stem; This part carries food and water through the plant., **c.** leaf; This part makes food for the plant., **d.** root; This part carries water from the soil to the plant.

Page 132

carrot, root; potato, root; parsley, leaf; celery, stem; lettuce, leaf; turnip, root; lettuce, leaf; asparagus, stem; beet, root

Page 133

Down: 1. sunlight, **2.** fruit, **6.** stem
Across: 1. seeds, **3.** flower, **4.** trunk, **5.** roots, **7.** leaf

Page 134

Drawings will vary.

Page 135

1. The root grows first., **2.** Roots, stems, and leaves grow from seeds.

Page 136

1. no, **2.** yes

Page 137

Correct order: Seed in pot, seed taking root, sprouting plant, and fully opened plant.; **1.** seeds, **2.** plants, **3.** flowers

Page 138

A. Plants need to be warm. The heater keeps them warm., B. Plants need air. Open windows let air in., C. Plants need sunlight. Glass lets the sunlight in., D. Plants need water. They are being watered.

Page 139

1. fish (rest are birds), **2.** beetle (rest are mammals), **3.** horse (rest are fish), **4.** bird (rest are reptiles), **5.** The horse is the largest animal on the page.

Page 140

Answers will vary.

Page 141

1. The birds ate the food with their beaks., **2.** The birds smelled the food and flew to the cup.

Page 142

1. S, **2.** F, **3.** W, **4.** W, **5.** W, **6.** F, **7.** F, **8.** W, **9.** S

Page 143

Students should color numbers 2, 3, 4, and 6.

Page 144

scales

Page 145

The reptile would most likely be in the sunlight on a cool day and in the shade on a hot day.

Page 146

a. fin, b. gills, c. tail

Page 147

gills, water, fins, tail, swim, shark, swim bladder

Page 148

Students should color the birds' wings and legs.

Page 149

Check students' work.

Page 151

Students should circle 1, 2, 3, 4, 7, 9, and 10. Students should mark an X on 5, 6, and 8.

Page 152

Drawings will vary.

Page 153

1. elephant, 2. seal, 3. whale, 4. eagle

Page 154

Students should color the deer and squirrel yellow, circle the 2 birds, color the 2 fish green, color the snake and turtle brown, and draw a square around the dragonfly.

Pages 155–156

1. insect, 2. bird, 3. reptile, 4. bird, 5. mammal, 6. insect, 7. fish, 8. reptile, 9. fish, 10. mammal

Page 157

1. water, food, 2. Drawings will vary. Hair will grow long if it is not cut., 3. The person in the middle should be circled. The person at the left should be colored.

Page 158

1.–3. Answers will vary., 4. no

Page 159

Answers will vary.

Page 160

1.–2. Answers will vary., 3. Growth can be measured by changing sizes of shoes and other clothing.

Page 161

1. eye, ear; 2. eye, ear, hand, nose; 3. eye, mouth, nose; 4. ear; 5. eye

Page 162

Answers will vary.

Page 163

Answers will vary.

Page 164

1. The answers to the question will depend upon the foods chosen. The students should describe their reactions to the new food or foods. They should also describe how it looks, feels, smells, tastes, and sounds when it is eaten., 2. The senses of sight, smell, touch, taste, and hearing should have been used.

Page 165

Students should put an **A** on the egg, the ham, the steak, the fish, the cheese, the turkey, and the milk. Students should put a **P** on the carrot, the nuts, the apple, the peas, the banana, the corn, the watermelon, and the orange.

Page 166

Students should color the milk, fish, apple, vegetables, nuts, and cereal.

Page 167

1. air, 2. rest, 3. play, 4. food, 5. water

Page 168

Students should put an X over A, D, and F.

Page 169

Answers will vary.

Page 170

Drawings will vary. Check students' work for accuracy.

Page 171

Students should circle C, D, E, and F. Students should put an X over A, B, and G.

Page 172

1. eyes, 2. eyes, 3. eyes, 4. both, 5. both, 6. both

www.svschoolsupply.com
© Steck-Vaughn Company

Answer Key
Science 1, SV 7933-2